Do not judge

Faye Reins

Copyright © 2024 by Faye Reins

All rights reserved.

No portion of this book may be reproduced in any form without written permission from the publisher or author, except as permitted by U.S. copyright law.

Contents

1. Chapter 1 — 1
2. Chapter 2 — 8
3. Chapter 3 — 16
4. Chapter 4 — 25
5. Chapter 5 — 34
6. Chapter 6 — 43
7. Chapter 7 — 51
8. Chapter 8 — 59
9. Chapter 9 — 68
10. Chapter 10 — 79
11. Chapter 11 — 88
12. Chapter 12 — 96
13. Chapter 13 — 105
14. Chapter 14 — 113
15. Chapter 15 — 122

16.	Chapter 16	130
17.	Chapter 17	140
18.	Chapter 18	150
19.	Chapter 19	162
20.	Chapter 20	176
21.	Chapter 21	191
22.	Chapter 22	201
23.	Chapter 23	212
24.	Chapter 24	220

Chapter 1

Time had run out for June, she was lost and the map she had sprawled out onto the seat beside her did not even show the road on the battered old sign outside. She needed to know where she was or else she would be late for the most important event of her twenty-seven years on this planet. She assessed the map again but it was to no avail Minaupi Road was not on her map.

"Arfghhhhhhhhhh!" she screamed as flung the worthless map out of her hands. "What kind of name was Minaupi anyway?"

Her phone had no signal and her Google map was rendered worthless as well. It could have been in Antarctica for the lack of signal she got from her phone.

Her mind wandered to her family, her parents and her sisters April and May. Her parents had named their daughters after the months in which they were born. June was the eldest followed by April. May was the baby of the family. If these were her last hours she would surely miss her family, they were really close.

June had always been the conscious one. The 'dependable' one, The reliable daughter. The one who her parents leaned on to solve all of her siblings' problems because she had the clearer head. She had always been careful in her choices. As a teenager she had managed her younger sisters' lives and money especially May's and had realised that she had a flair for management. So when she graduated from secondary school she had decided that she would be a management executive.

After graduating from university with a degree in Management studies, June had gotten employment with the Hemusk Organisation as a junior assistant in the Marketing department. Five months ago she had been awarded her MSc in Business Management and Marketing after doing it part time for two years. She had her whole career ahead of her, and today she had been offered the position of her dreams: Senior Marketing Officer in the marketing department. She loved her job and now as a senior officer, she had her freedom to develop products and execute them plus she managed the twenty-eight other members of the department. She did not hate her colleagues but 20 of them were over forty and had not moved with the times.

She got out of the vehicle, the sun was setting, and it would be dark soon. She looked around her; there was a huge expanse of green brush for miles. The dirt road she was on lead to a desert of nothingness. How could she have veered off the motorway and ended up here? About twenty minutes ago, she had decided to look for a small inn or B&B where she could rent a room for the night, her plans seemed alright until she took a turn to the left and got off the motorway. Somehow she could not navigate her way back onto the M26.

She got back into the 35-year-old truck that she had borrowed from the clerk at the gas station in the last town after her two front tyres had been punctured because he had put down metal grates in front of her rental when she was moving out of the gas station.

She made a decision.

"Okay, since I am here I will just keep on driving," she said to herself, "I am sure some one from this wasteland will be around soon."

The engine started with a hushed tone as if it was expecting her not to continue. She eased down the dusty road bumping along with the potholes. Tomorrow she was expected to be in Edinburgh but if she could not make it she would lose everything, everything she had worked hard for the last six years.

However, today she was going to be late for her big chance if she could not find her way out of this empty space. The sun had gone down but a few embers of light still illuminated the cloudy sky. June kept going along her route hoping to see some life form before it got too dark. Suddenly, a large deluge of rain exploded from the heavens. A rainstorm!

"No!" she screamed banging onto her steering wheel. She knew that travelling alone would have been treacherous but not like this not now when things were finally going her way, when she had decided to let her hair down and to relax and to take a chance. She had no qualms about an adventure but not when she finally had her dream job.

The heavy rain made her visibility poor so she had to inch across the horrible road that was now a spit of gluey soil, not fit for even a worm to crawl in. She had been driving for nearly an hour in the downpour when she saw a light in the distance. She inched toward it but soon found out that there was not direct road to get to it. June still tried to manoeuvre the old truck through the dense bush and suddenly she heard pop. The truck could not move. She tried in vain but it was stuck.

"Arghhhhhhhh!" she screamed and banged her hands on the steering wheel. She got out in the fading light and surveyed the truck. She noticed that some branches were wrapped around the tyres and mud was everywhere. What was she to do? She gathered her stuff, her overnight case, brief case and handbag out on the truck. Her shoes were already ruined by the mud, her hair and clothes were drenched but at least she would not have to sleep in the dirty musty truck. She navigated her way treacherously through the dense bush to the light.

She trudged slowly and carefully along a wooded and grassy path that she could not see clearly because of the weather and the fading light. Finally, she saw the cottage, it was just beyond a clump of trees. She just had to go a little further and then she would be safe. She stopped for a minute safe! What if a rapist lived in that cottage or drug dealers? Come to think of it, why was this cottage so excluded? She stopped and took a deep breath what now? Either she trudged back to the truck and hoped to find it in this mess or she went to the cottage. June offered a silent prayer and ventured forth. This day was the full of first times. She had made more risky decisions today than she had in her entire life.

She made it to the front door. There was a light burning in the well-built cottage. It was no poor man's outfit from the feel of the wood beneath her fingers this was expertly crafted she was even more curious as to who lived here! She pounded a bit louder but no one came forth she peered through the window next to the door and saw a roaring fireplace at least inside was warm. The place looked well kept and large. She knocked the door again, still no response she turned the doorknob and it opened.

She walked in slowly scanning her new surroundings. It was a new place. The furnishings were exquisite like those from the glossy fashion magazines. The living area flowed into large open kitchen/ dining area. The bar stools propped in front of the divider of the two areas had plush brown leather seats fitted into real deep mahogany wood. The whole place had woodcarvings from the sparkling wooden floors that covered the entire area to the huge wooden pillars that stood imposingly in the small foyer leading to the stairs. June had always loved such a natural looking place but it was pricey.

She scanned to her left and saw a short flight of stairs, which probably led to the bedrooms upstairs. She placed her things on the mat at the door, hoping they would not wet the polished wooden floor. June decided to ascend the stairwell, maybe who ever lived here was upstairs she glanced at the huge clock over the fire place it was barely 8 o'clock. She arrived on the landing. There were five doors, two on each side, directly opposite each other and the final one directly across from where she was standing.

She knocked on the first door on her right but after no response she opened it and realised that it was a den, with a huge oak desk and a sofa lining the left wall and books lining the other wall; sadly, it was also empty of human life. She did the same to the door adjacent; it was a bedroom, immaculately furnished but also empty. The four rooms, three of which were bedrooms, were all empty except the last door, which she had not entered. She opened it slowly so far no one had answered her calls.

She entered what was definitely the master suite. The huge king sized bed dominated the room with its mahogany four-poster stands. There was an armchair, a Plasma TV, a small balcony off on the right, plus one of the largest walk-in closets that she had ever seen, and she could make out clothes hanging there and to be more specific male clothing. It was a man's room, from the rich burgundy sheets to the deep mahogany furniture. Plus the male scent made that fact real.

The door adjacent to the bed was open and light streamed through it. She walked tentatively towards it. She stopped just shy of the door and called out once more,

"Hello? Is anyone there? Hello?" no response.

As she stepped into the room, she could hear a shower running and some other muffled sounds. The noise, it sounded like singing, she smiled, the voice was quiet sultry and deep and definitely male! She stopped; she didn't want to walk in on a man in his shower. What if he came out naked, now that would be embarrassing! The best decision would be to wait downstairs. She turned and started to creep slowly toward the bedroom door. She was almost to the door when she heard,

'Stop!' she froze and turned around slowly.

She came face to face with the sultry voice's owner. He was standing stark naked in the bathroom door way. She looked straight at the chest in front of her and then she looked down automatically, which elicited more shock from her at the absolute beauty of the body that was exposed in front of her. This was an elite specimen of the male anatomy.

June looked up guiltily; her face flushed red with the shock at seeing a man naked and a really well proportioned one at that. His olive skin was glistening from his shower; it was tanned and looked smooth and lean all over. June's eyes travelled slowly up his frame from his strong muscled feet to his well defined chest and then to his face. She was jolted out of her admiration by a very angry face staring at her. His piercing brown eyes were mesmerizing.

"What are you doing in my house?" spoke the Adonis before her. She noted that his voice was deep and heavily accented. His handsome face was clouded by a scowl and his brown eyes pierced into her.

June stood there speechless, her voice had deserted her, her eyes were shining like a deer caught in headlamps and although her brain told her lips to speak they refused to move.

"I asked you a question?" the man made no move to cover himself she noted and that kept her mesmerized. He took a few steps forward, held her arms, and shook her. This helped her come out of her temporary paralysis.

"I-I-I ju-st wanted a place to sleep," she stumbled out. Her voice was shaking through nervousness.

"Who are you? Who sent you?" he seemed very angry now and his scowl deepened.

"I- I "she blurted out, cluelessly.

He shook her again and his wet jet-black hair sprayed water all over her. "Answer me woman!"

"No one sent me, I am lost and I saw the light!" she ventured feeling like a schoolgirl caught skipping class.

He stretched for his towel wrapped it around his waist all the while dragging her with his free hand. She was like a rag doll as he dragged her out of the room and down the stairs.

Please vote and comment and thanks for reading!

Let me hear your thoughts!

Chapter 2

A pic of Giannis Tsimitellis a Greek actor....I can totally see him playing Dmitri, he carries the arrogant look off elegantly...!

"You're hurting me!" she screamed as she tripped on the stairs. He ignored her and only stopped at the front door where her rain-drenched things lay on the floor. He put her to stand in front of him and started to go through her bags. Her senses started to come back as he started to throw her things all over the floor.

'You can't do that!" she said struggling to pull her purse from him.

His obvious 6 ft plus height and muscled body was no match for her 5 ft 6" frame. He sidestepped her efforts and emptied her bag onto the floor. Her purse, cosmetic case, pens, tissue pads all crashed to the floor. She rushed to pick up a rolling lipstick, by the time she had gathered the strewn items he was delving through her case. Now her clothes were scattered all over the floor in front of him. Her efforts to pull them out of his hands yielded no fruit as he shoved her aside like a sack of potatoes and continued his search. June did not give up and scrambled to gather her stuff.

'Hey leave that!' she screamed and pulled her panties out of his grasp. Finally, he stood up and to her horror she realised, that he still had her purse.

He was now taking out her cards and reading them. When he reached her drivers' license, he held it up and looked from it to her.

'Satisfied!' she said trying to grab it from him but he held her arm away from him.

'Let me go you freak!' she kicked him and attempted to pull her purse from him but somehow she only held his towel in her hands. He had the gall to stand there totally naked and continue reading through her stuff as if, nothing untoward had just happened.

'You're crazy,' she finally said and flung his towel at him.

He caught it, wrapped it around his waist and now stood in front of her ensuring that she resembled the photograph he held "So June Stapleton, tell me what you are doing here?"

She was angry now how dare he treat her like a vagrant.

"I already told you I was lost." She repeated stonily through her clenched teeth.

"This is a remote area, how did you get here?' his gaze was unrelenting as he stared at her waiting for a response. He made her so nervous.

"A- a- truck,' she stuttered, not fully recovered from his harsh treatment of her. She felt like an errant teenager who had been caught climbing out of the window at an all girls boarding school ran by nuns. He raised his eyebrow disbelievingly and then opened the front door. He stepped out onto the porch and looked out into the black and stormy night.

"So where is it?" he was looking at her now. This man was the ultimate suspicious Joe, why was he so afraid? He stepped back into the house and shut the door, the scowl on his face deepened as he assessed her attire.

"Listen mister, I am wet, hungry and tired, the old truck is somewhere behind those woods. As you can plainly see, I am also dirty from trudging through thick woods because this cottage was the only light I saw for miles. If I had known that you would be so hostile I would have slept in the truck instead."

"That is still an option."

June looked at the speaker of those cold words in shock. The man had the audacity to say that to her after all this. What kind of monster was he? June lost it she picked up a nearby vase and hurled it at him but he sidestepped as it crashed into the wall behind him. There was utter silence for a moment except for the rain pelting on the cottage roof.

June was heaving; this creature in front of her was callous. He stood there menacingly ready to deliver cruelty. He was a man who yielded power and arrogance. He expected to be obeyed and she hated him in that moment. She wanted him gone. Why couldn't she just have found a simple person who would want to offer her a bed for the night?

They studied each other like opponents sizing up the competition. His eyes changed and he dropped his shoulders as if admitting defeat. He walked towards her and stared into her eyes as he said,

"I will give you a room for the night, you will leave in the morning, but I still do not trust you."

He picked up her travel case and walked up the stairs. For the second time that evening, June was left speechless. Did that brute just offer her a bed or a prison cell?

She turned round and belatedly followed him up the stairs; he had placed her in the room closest to his: control she thought. She entered the room to find him unpacking her case, no correction, searching through it. He had her stuff strewn all over the bed as he searched through her clothes.

"What is it with you? I am not spy, you already went through my wallet, and you know where I work, live, what I do, so get over yourself?' she rushed to pull her panties out of his hand.

'I don't even know your name and if I wasn't so criminal I would not have announced myself when I first entered this place!"

He merely stopped his search and stood satisfied after placing her white thong back in the suitcase. He looked at her strangely as if concluding that she did not have any weapons. He strode out of the room. June stood there for a few moments lost as to what to do. She was wet tired and hungry.

She decided she needed to change her clothes. She went to the en suite; it was gorgeous with a huge bath tub and adjoining shower. It was white with clean lines accentuated by a sable brown décor. June decided to lock the bedroom door but to her utter amazement, it was already locked. She turned the knob, it did not budge. He had locked her in!

Who was he and why was he so suspicious, he could be a drug dealer or worse an assassin but something about him showed that he was neither, he was ruthless that much she had gathered; her arms still bore his prints. June still positioned the desk chair against the door for some form of protection.

June sat on the bathtub edge, what could she deduce about her captor?

He had a Spanish accent so he wasn't British but he was rich, this room alone had more wealth that her entire savings, the question is why was he in such a secluded cottage? Was he escaping from someone or hiding from something? She questioned all these things in her mind, as she tidied her clothes. She at least would get a bath. The water was glorious; it warmed her chilled bones and brought some life back to body. She put on a pair of sweats and a tank top. She blow dried her hair but decided to leave it loose. She was hungry and she was not going to remain locked in this room until the next day. She started to pound on the door and shout.

"Hello! Hello!" she screamed loudly, "Open the door!"

After what seemed like an eternity, her captor opened the door. He did not even look at her but turned and walked down the stairway. He entered the kitchen area; from one glance around, she noted that he had cleaned up the broken vase and that her briefcase was on the dining room table wide open. The limit of this man was too much to bear! She went to her case. He had studied every document in her case.

"Here is a sandwich and there is some hot coffee in the pot."

She whirled to face him and cocked her eyebrows, "Satisfied that I'm who I say I am?"

He did not even acknowledge that he heard her, instead he poured himself a cup of coffee and stalked off to the sofa and flickered on the TV, she was too hungry to go after him.

"What hospitable service, your mother sure would be proud that she raised a son with no manners!" she said loudly.

The slight twitch of his jaw was the only reaction he gave to her words. She poured herself some caffeine and ate hungrily while he watched Headline news. That man was so handsome and visually appealing but he had the personality of a truck driver.

He was now fully clothed in a pair of grey sweats that dazzled with his eyes and a white v neck shirt.

He had beautifully chiselled cheek bones with ooh so full lips what was she thinking, this man could be a murderer for all she knew but just looking at him sitting so tense on the sofa, she knew he wasn't. He was strong and foreboding but he was not such an evil person. She did not want to alarm him any further so she quietly washed her dishes, gathered up her stuff, and made her way up the stairs. To her surprise, he was following her.

"What is it with you?" She turned around, "You haven't even told me your name."

He seemed to sign off, and then he said in hushed tones "Dmitri."

"Dmitri, what a nice name for a monster." she whispered and saw his lips twisted into a sneer.

"Let me make myself clear, I do not know what your problem is but I did not deliberately seek you out, I was genuinely lost and stumbled upon this place and as you well know this area is vacant."

"I believe you June Stapleton but no one can be too careful these days." His eyes were blank what had happened to make him so cynical and sad. She pitied him, her life had been filled with rules, but she was happy; he looked like he had few scenes of happiness in his life.

"Well thank you for escorting me to the door but I will be fine and for your information I will be locking the door from the inside."

He said nothing just put his hands into his pocket. She entered her room astounded as to what had happened to Dmitri to make him so sad. As she closed the door she heard the lock turn, that man was too stubborn for his own good. The door had a dead bolt lock on the inside. She turned it and placed the lone chair behind the door again. He was right we could not be too safe these days.

June remembered that she needed to call Jay to tell him of her dilemma, but as she dug through her handbag, she realised that her cell phone was missing, because Dmitri must have taken it. Finally, after so many long sleepless nights, she was handed the biggest account of her life and everything was going wrong. How would she inform her assistant that he would need to commence the presentation without her if she had no way of contacting him? That dratted man called Dmitri was the cause of these new turn of events in her already horrendous day.

First of all, all flights at Augier Airport had been either delayed or cancelled due to an impending thunderstorm, so she had decided to drive to Spakane instead.

Mistake number one.

She sat down on the bed exasperated glancing casually around the room, for a bedroom with all modern amenities it was surely lacking in the most essential, a telephone. She flopped back onto the crisp sheets going back over the day's tragic events.

Then the doodle head, Morris, at the gas station had punctured two of her tyres while he had been washing them, and in her haste or maybe shock she had taken his ancient truck. He had promised that 'Old Misty' was the most reliable vehicle in town.

Mistake number two.

She had been driving to the next airport to get a flight but what was supposed to be a three-hour drive had turned into a nightmare. She had taken the wrong turn along the plentiful dirt country roads. The map which Morris had supplied her with was outdated.

That was mistake number three.

After getting stuck in the ditch with old Misty she had stumbled upon this house and entered it.

Mistake number four.

Now she was stuck in a room, in a house belonging to the coldest hearted man on the planet.

Mistake number five.

How would she get back tomorrow, would he even help her? She was tired but she did not want to sleep. She needed to contact Jay tonight and it would be Dmitri's fault if he felt that she was bothering him. She undid the deadbolt of the door only to realise that it was still locked. The bastard had still locked her in, even after researching her! The gall of that man, he was insufferable. June started to pound on the door loudly and then she began to scream like her life depended on it...well technically her job did! She could hear him bounding up the stairs.

"Stop it!" he shouted from the other side of the door.

"When you open this door I will!" she rebutted. She almost fell forward as the door was forcefully swung open. She righted herself and fixed her clothes before staring into the coldest pair of eyes she had ever seen.

"Okay, Mr. Suspicious Joe," she began counting on the fingers of her left hand,

"Listen carefully to what I am about to say:

1. I am not here to kill you in your sleep although by your attitude you deserve it.

2. I detest the fact that you feel the need to lock me in when I am totally harmless and I mean look at my size compared to yours.

3. I need my mobile phone right now."

She finished her list and put her hands on her hips. The lout had the audacity to smirk. June was so furious she raised her hand to slap him but he caught her hand before it struck his face.

"Not harmless?" he said sneeringly.

Chapter 3

June lost control and kicked out as she struggled to free her captured arm. He twisted her arm behind her and she fought him with all her strength. She kicked and pushed and somehow they ended up on the floor with Dmitri straddling her as she lay on her back with her arms crossed over her chest and held down by his hands. Her chest was heaving from the struggle as Dmitri sat there calm as the breeze.

"Unhand me, you lout!" she screamed, as she tried to get her breath back.

"Calm yourself, woman!" he said forcefully. June stayed still for a few moments as her captor made no move to release her.

"Okay, all I want is my phone!" she pleaded to the monster holding her down.

"I will release you only if you promise to behave yourself." He responded calmly.

Did he think she was a petulant five year old, who needed to be corrected? June wanted to explode but one look at Dmitri's face prevented her from doing so, so she held her tongue in check and said meekly,

"I promise as long as I get my phone." He got off her and stretched out his hand to help her get off the floor. She scrambled to her feet totally ignoring his hand.

He walked down the stairs and she followed him silently wishing she could give him a swift kick in the derriere and see him rolling down the stairs; the thought brought a smile to her lips as she descended after him. If only she wondered, she did not know what happened to her but her foot was raised and she just kicked him then and there. Dmitri stumbled forward but regained his balance quickly as he clutched to the banister. June was smiling wickedly, he so deserved that a pity though he was not flat on his face. Her captor turned around with eyes full of fire. June straightened her shoulders and just brushed past him saying,

'You know you deserved that!' as she sprinted down the remaining stairs.

She spotted her phone on the sofa next to where he had probably been seated until she had called him upstairs. The television was showing the weather report so she attuned her ears. The weather man stated that the storm would soon be over and advised that only a few scattered showers were possible tomorrow.

'Great,' she said turning around to see Dmitri casually leaning on the banister.

'I will be out of your hair tomorrow, sleep well!' she sang sweetly as she swept past him and bounded up the stairs.

She liked having the last word and the fact that he did not follow her showed that he had relaxed enough to accept her presence. She bolted her door and sat Indian style on the bed to call Jay.

'Hello,' he answered groggily.

'Jay, are you asleep it's barely 10 pm?' she inquired

'Just tired,.....June? Where are you? I have been waiting all afternoon?' he demanded

'My wonderful Jay, I am stuck in Spakane and from the look of the weather; I will not be coming out until late tomorrow morning.' There was complete silence on the other side of the call.

'Jay, Jay you there?' she asked worriedly.

'June, the meeting is at 9 am tomorrow, you have to be here!' his voice was high pitched and he seemed to be shouting.

'It seems I won't be so you will need to start of the proceedings I—'

Jay cut her off rushing in to add, 'No, no, June I can't do this on my own this is your baby!'

'Breathe a minute Jay, you can, in fact you have to, we have no other choice, I am stuck here.'

She could hear the panic in her assistant's voice as he rumbled on decrying their present situation and his impending 'promotion'. He was a good worker but in the seven months that they had worked together, he had never led a meeting of such a magnitude but he had the ability. He was timid but very forceful in a small group. If she had not seen his potential she would have had him relocated to another department months ago. Now, he had to shine and she would be screwed if he failed.

'Come on Jay, you can do this.....' her voice trailed off as he sighed for the umpteenth time.

'Oh no June, I need you here, can I send a helicopter, a private jet? Please don't do this to me now I am not prepared!' he was hyperventilating.

'Be a man Jay!' she spoke strongly as she got off the bed and walked to the window, it was still pouring outside, and she hoped the weather man would be correct for her sake and her job.

'If I believed that you could not do this then I would have told you to cancel; now you listen and listen well.'

'But June, I can't do this, it's your presentation, oh no!' she heard a plopping sound and figured that he had rather ungracefully flopped onto the bed.

'Now listen, you have the presentation notes right?'

'Yes' came the soft reply

'Plus we went through the presentation yesterday and there no glitches right?'

'I need a drink!' Jay finally said defeatingly.

'No Jay you have to be level headed......... it all depends on you now.'

'I don't want it to!' his voice was resigned but she knew he had made the decision to take this on. He was now trying to fight it like a man hanging onto straw.

'Okay, listen to me, we have been working on this for two months now right?'

'Yes!' came the feeble reply

'Good you know every step as well as me, 'kay?'

'Yeah,'

'Great, so now all you need to do is go over the presentation tonight, everything is on the pen drive, you have a copy plus there is a back up CD so just go through it, you will do fine Jay, I have the utmost confidence in you.'

'You really think I can do this?' he asked softly

'I know you can, Jay you are my assistant if you weren't good you would not be working with me.' She said confidently knowing that he valued her opinions greatly.

'Thanks June, that means a lot to me.' He accepted sounding a bit more calm.

They went over the presentation twice; she gave him tips on where he should pause and how he should maintain eye contact especially with the Chairman. Jay was brilliant and she knew he would do a fine job on her behalf.

'Good now just shape up and go over the presentation tomorrow, go to bed now and have a some good sleep. I know it will be okay just explain the reason for my absence on the weather situation and I will join you later.......okay.' she tried to be reassuring as possible.

'June, I will not let you down.' His voice was beaming now, with renewed confidence. June smiled, art least the presentation was one less worry she had to deal with tonight.

'You had better not,' she said jokingly 'I know you have the ability to do it, so be brave and have a good night's rest, I will see you tomorrow.'

'Oh June you are indeed the best, see you tomorrow.'

'Goodnight Jay.'

'Night June.'

She closed her phone and stared out at the stormy night, this was an important meeting but she was positive that Jay could do a good job. It would be the first time in her five years at the company that she would miss a presentation., she was pretty hands on and liked to do her work herself but she was forced to release it because of the weather, what it had in store for her she did not know but she hoped that it was a positive sign.

She had not had a vacation in two years. Not because she could not but she had not wanted to go anywhere. Her work was her essence; it completed her and made her feel important. She would sleep and hope that she could leave here by six a.m., she did not want to be to late for the presentation. She trusted Jay but it was still her baby, she had fought had for the deal and when it had come her way she had relished in the fact that she was the youngest person: woman or man to be working on such a deal with Gyrish Incorporated.

June finally conceded that she could only do so much tonight. The rain would stop and she would be on her way out of here tomorrow. However she still had to deal with the host from the crypt.

She needed to be alert for Dmitri, he had not ascended and was probably still doing a background check on her. What would he find, she had a modest two bedroom flat in Bershire, a nice suburban place. She lived alone and was a workaholic with no boyfriend or husband. She was stuck in a rut, no a drought. Her work had been her number one priority and looking back she had not had time to date or even entertain a guy.

The last person she had been out with was two years ago and he had been an upcoming attorney. Grant Patterson was pompous and egotistical. His only reason for dating her was that 'she was from good stock'. She had dumped his behind as soon as he had uttered the words. He wanted a wife to improve his image since he was vying for partner in his firm. The louse was handsome but cold and calculating. He had told her that he was the best man in town that she would ever find and her response had been to tell him that if he was the best then the town had to be surely disappointing.

She changed into her night clothes and snuggled under the lush satin sheets. Whoever had furnished and decorated this place has very expensive tastes was it his lover, wife? She wondered about him. She stilled her self that she had to stay awake but as soon as her head hit the pillow, she was fast sleep.

The next day she could not move, she was cold all over and her throat felt closed up. She tried to speak but her throat was so raw she could not, she tried to open her eyes, but they were too heavy. Her whole body ached.

Was she dead?

Did Dmitri kill her?

She could feel a warm cloth on her forehead and a voice was telling her to open her eyes. It sounded strange she could not focus because she was hurting all over what was wrong with her? She felt her head being lifted and some liquid was being pushed inside her mouth, she could not swallow because her throat was like a scorching desert. She felt herself being sucked into a vacuum and she was too weak to resist it.

Dmitri stood staring at the woman on the bed below him. She had been like this for the past two days. Her fever had been over 100 degrees. She had been having cold sweats and coughing profusely. It seems her trudge through the woods in the rain had done her in. Luckily, he had checked on her about nine the previous morning, and found her writhing on her bed.

He was still unsure why she had not gone toward the little village, which was nine miles in the opposite direction. Instead, she had fallen onto his doorstep to disturb his tranquillity. His guards had found her ancient truck yesterday morning, lodged in mud and in thick brush. His body guards had said that the plates belonged to a gas station owner from the previous town. His men had found the owner and it seemed that she had exchanged her rental car for the old truck because she needed new tyres.

In essence she had been telling the truth. He knew she was who she had said she was, but in his position, he knew the lengths people had gone through to penetrate his life. He could take no more chances, once was lesson enough.

He had gotten a private physician to visit. It was confirmed that she had a cold but her body was tired and it was struggling with the infection. He had moved her to his room because he wanted to take care of her. He could have hired a nurse but this spitfire had turned him on from the first night they met. She had been spunky and on fire. She needed a soak in the tub to relieve the heat within her body.

Her body was exquisite. She had full ripe breasts, just longing to be suckled by him. Her hips were well proportioned. She was by no means skinny but full everywhere. He had never been attracted to women like her before but holding her, bathing her he knew that how supple she would be in his arms. Her legs were long and she had pretty ankles and such beautiful toes. Her hair was short and black. If she let it grow, she would surely be a catwalk model.

He knew she was a professional from his one phone call he got all the information he needed about her. She came from a close knit family was the eldest all three girls who were all named after months of the year. He wondered why? She moved onto her side exposing her left breast. He had left her naked under the sheets because she was sweating so much. He had never had a woman in his bed without having sex with her but June Stapleton was a first, she had barged into his life and taken it over.

No one had ever stood up to him but she had and seemed very unafraid to face him. Most people were afraid of him because he knew his demeanour was unapproachable plus his 6 ft 4" height did little to aid matters but

June had stood up to him from the onset. Something flittered in his gut. He wanted her and he intended to have her. After all, he was nursing her back to good health. He fixed her sheet and left to get more warm tea for her to drink.

Chapter 4

June opened her eyes, she felt tired and weak. Her mouth felt like cotton wool. Her limbs felt like jelly but she could barely remember where she was, she looked up and saw Dmitri seated on the armchair near the bed. His head bowed while he was reading a magazine, her memory flooded back to their first encounter. Her cheeks flushed he was a monster and what was he doing in her room. The last she remembered was falling asleep after he locked her in.

What was he doing here?

What time was it?

She needed to leave. She tried to sit up and moaned. Dmitri stood up and walked toward her. He sat on the bed and touched her forehead,

"You're feeling better I see," he said and for the first time he smiled and the sheer beauty of the man blew her away. She flinched at his touch.

"What are you doing here?" she asked her throat feeling raw and painful.

He continued to smile while touching her throat, "You have been sick,"

"Sick? I have never been sick in my life, what did you do to me?"

He raised an eyebrow, now whom was being suspicious? "You have had a high fever and almost succumbed to hypothermia."

She did not want to believe him but her body was too weak and aching for her to deny that he spoke the truth.

"I need to use the bathroom," she said hoping he would leave but to her astonishment, he pulled away the covers to reveal her naked body and gathered her into his arms.

She screamed," Let me go!" trying to cover herself.

"No need for modesty now June I have seen it all for the last three days." Dmitri spoke wickedly as he looked down at her.

"Three days! I have been sick for three days!" She squirmed in his arms as he brought her to the toilet and put her on it.

She had modesty and she bowed her head as she stared at her feet; did he want her to ask him to leave?

"I will leave you to it when you're done just call me... He turned to leave but before he said, "Just look at it as if we're even." he left her alone in the spacious bathroom.

It was then that she realised that she was in a different room. June was in shock, this callous man had taken care of her for three days? He was different though, he seemed happier not the monster she had encountered three days ago. She put her head in her hands, she was screwed, and her boss would surely fire her over this she had no way of contacting her or vice versa. Was there a search party for her? Her parents would surely be worried. She had not been sick since she was a child. She had taken ample care to ensure that she never fell sick, because her job demanded it.

She tried to lever herself up and head to the shower because her skin felt clammy. It was difficult but she made it by holding the wall and scrambling on her knees. She would not give him the satisfaction of calling him for assistance. She got into the shower and turned on the spray, ooh this felt good but she so weak she had to lean against the wall. Before she knew it Dmitri was there holding the soap.

"Why didn't you call me?"

She gave him a glare and he smiled totally reading her expression.

"It's okay I've seen it all already." she flushed but he scrubbed her down efficiently. She was too feeble to oppose his gestures. He dried her and carried her to the bed that had fresh blue satin sheets. He dressed her in a large t-shirt of his and dried her hair while she leaned against his solid chest. She remained quiet while he dressed her, too embarrassed to speak.

He fitted the sheets around her as he would a five year old.

"I'll get you some thing to eat, you must be famished."

"Thank you," she whispered hoarsely,

He smiled, "You're welcome" was all he said as he disappeared out of the room.

June scrambled to get up, she had to get out of here and get her hands on her mobile. She saw his coat hanging on the hook across the room. She searched it but no mobile, she crawled to the bureau and all she found were his clothes. He found her on her knees crawling to the bed.

He put down the tray and picked her up.

"Just where are you going to?" he said almost lovingly as he carried her like a child.

"Please I need to contact my family, I need my phone. I need it please!" she pleaded with him as he placed her under the covers.

"Your family knows that you are okay."

"What! How?" she was puzzled.

"Your parents have been phoning regularly to check up on you, they know that you were sick and well then…," he said nonchalantly letting his voice drift away as if he did this every day.

"But… How?" she was still unsure how he had contacted her family.

"Your mobile is a pretty busy one; your family seem to be concerned?"

She sat up straight, "Wouldn't you be? Where's my phone?" he took it out of his back pocket and handed it to her, she hurriedly dialled her parent's number as he stood watching,

"Mom, yes, yes, I'm fine, no I am feeling much better," she breathed deeply answering her mother's rapid fire questioning.

Dmitri could not hear what her mother was saying but by the way, she was glancing at him every few seconds, she knew that he was part of the conversation. He retreated to the bathroom to give them some privacy as he tidied it up.

"Honey we are so happy that you're recovering so fast your young man is a keeper."

"My what?"

"No need to be shy honey he told us everything how you two met, we are so happy for you?"

"But Mom?" Her mother was ranting on and not letting her get a word in edge wise.

"Honey we know you love your work but this sickness just shows that you need to relax stop trying to save the world!

"Mom...?" June was lost.

"I know I love you get better take all your time to rest and we love you." Her mother's voice was cheery and light.

"I love you too mom." her mother rang off leaving her with more questions than answers.

She called Jay next.

"Hey, you're feeling better I see."

'Oh Jay I am so sorry about this how did the presentation go?'

'It was cool Mr. Hamilton was so impressed,' he thoroughly appreciated all our hard work.

"He wasn't mad about my absence?' she asked worriedly.

'No, he totally understood especially after your boyfriend spoke to him,'

"My boyfriend?' Dmitri had been hard at work messing with her life.

'Yeah he had a very long conversation with him and the old chap was a darling afterwards. He even said that you were in need of some time off.'

"Really?" her monosyllabic responses were all she could muster as shock seeped through her brain.

She rang off and spoke to her boss next, she took a deep breath,

'Mr. Hamilton, I am so sorry about this...'

'Hi, June there's nothing to worry about Jay is capable of handling this, you have done all the ground work anyway, so how are you feeling?'

He was actually asking about her health she was shocked.

"I'm not all there yet still weak but I should be fine by tomorrow, I will fly down to Spakane first thing in the morning?'

"No!" he vehemently rejected, "You take the next two weeks off, plus you are entitled to a vacation."

June was speechless.

"Well dear get better and see you soon."

She sat there holding the phone with her mouth open as Dmitri walked back into the room, she stared at him pointedly,

"Just what did you say to everyone?"

"What do you mean?" he said carrying the tray to her.

"Everyone thinks that you—-that I—- that we are a couple?" She finally managed.

He had the audacity to look sheepish... "It was the best explanation that I could give, your mother would have been mortified to know that I was a complete stranger to her daughter."

"But you are, I barely know anything about you but you have rearranged my life in three days."

"You should be grateful from what I have learned you have not had a break for a while maybe this was your body saying that it needed rest."

"Thanks Doc" was the cold response from her, the soup was delicious, she drunk it quickly but he stopped her.

"Slow, your body has not had much in it for a few days so take it slowly." he guided the mug to her mouth. She closed her mouth and pulled away.

"I am not a child!" she screamed, "Stop trying to control me, I can drink on my own!" he stood up straight put his hands on his hips and smiled at her.

"The tiger is unleashed I can safely conclude that you are back to your old self." he walked away.

"Wait, I'm sorry but I hate people trying to interfere, obviously you were thinking of my interest, thank you." the words were torn from her.

He turned around and his eyes pierced hers,

"You're welcome, now you need some rest."

He was right she was still tired but she needed some more answers.

"Yes but first tell me who you are?"

He was contemplating what to say to her. He had a cover story prepared but she added, "I think you owe me the whole truth since you know very detail about my life!"

She was intuitive he realised, but he was going to lie. He was not comfortable releasing information about himself but this time he would tell her who he was, albeit partly, because she was right. Plus he wanted her so badly, his loins ached every time he touched. Her looked at her in his shirt and watched her nipples tight against the cloth. He hardened.

"My name is Dmitri Bergano, I am Sicilian."

"Sicilian? What are you doing here in a remote Cumbria village?" she asked curiously.

"I'm house sitting for my boss." Came the smooth response.

"Your boss? Is he Sicilian too?" June was unsure whether she was being told the truth or a well-crafted story.

"He is an American, he recently built this place and sent me here to oversee the final furnishings and to report to him if it is up to standard." Dmitri could see that June was looking at him sceptically. He needed to give her the punchline now to make his story plausible.

"So what do you and your boss do for a living?" June asked highly suspicious now.

"I am from Sicily and you know what they say about us?" He let the question hang in the air.

June looked at the eastern balcony which had a breathtaking view of the morning sunrise and the mountains which were looking so calm and inviting. She was in a secluded cottage in Cumbria with a Sicilian stranger who had rearranged her life in three days and was very suspicious and sensitive about his privacy.

She looked at Dmitri again as he was staring at her cautiously.

Everyone knew what suspicious people did in Sicily and she realised that it all fit.

Could he really be in the mafia? It did fit in with the hidden away building and his attitude toward her when they first met? His searching through her cases and her bag like she was a criminal.

His phone rang to break the still air.

"Excuse me." He said moving to the open balcony.

He was rattling off to the caller in Greek.

One of the receptionists at her company was of Greek heritage and based on her limited knowledge of the language he was speaking Greek.

Why would a Sicilian know Greek?

Was he telling her the truth? It did fit.

He was now speaking in English. She could not hear what he was saying properly but she did her name mentioned.

He was coming back into the room and June pretended to be drinking some water.

"Make sure the shipment is delivered today. It is vital that it is collected tomorrow. I will be awaiting your call on the final dispatch." Dmitri ended the call and came toward her.

She swung her legs off the bed and flinched when he held her arm.

" I just wanted to go to the bathroom" June said softly, she needed time to think.

"Let me help you," He offered with a smile.

"No I am stronger now, thank you." June was petrified of the man.

June stood up and made her way to the bathroom holding on the wall for support. She leaned against the door and locked it firmly. She was being taken care of by a man in the mafia. She did not want to even guess what the 'shipment' was?

Oh my Goodness she thought. How was she going to leave this place in one piece and not in a body bag?

She was definitely going to be nice to Dmitri from now on ... it would be hard since he was such a jerk but...he did take care of her so she had to be grateful somewhat?

Chapter 5

June was resting when Dmitri came in to check on her.

"How are you feeling now?" he asked coming to sit beside her. He had brought in some warm ginger tea. June's heart started to explode. His nearness was doing strange things to her body. She was feeling tingly all over. She tried to sip the tea slowly as they remained in quiet. Dmitri was staring at her and she was looking everywhere but at him.

"How old are you?" she blurted out.

"Why do you want to know?" he countered staring at her intensely with his brown eyes.

"You never answered my question," he smiled.

"I am thirty-two."

Wow, he was five years older than she was.

He bent to take the empty cup from her and she could smell the masculine scent of his body.

She inhaled and he looked at her, for a moment, they were suspended in eternity and bent his face toward her. As his lips captured her own, her mind was screaming no but her body was getting warm all over. His lips were full and so soft that she opened up her mouth for his tongue, which slipped, into her mouth. As their tongues mingled, June spiralled; her hands pulled him closer to her.

This was pure bliss, she had never been kissed by a man like this before, he was her nectar, he slowly released her mouth as she opened her eyes and let her hands fall away from his face. His eyes were full of passion and she could feel the heat coming off him. She shyly lowered her eyelashes. She had never wantonly given herself to a man like that before. He picked up the tray and walked out without saying a word.

June exhaled what had come over her. What must he think of her? She was too tired to move although she wanted to high tail it out of the room. Instead, she sank under the covers and promptly fell asleep. She woke up a few hours later. It must be afternoon. She had no idea of time.

She needed to get out of here, sick or not. She scrambled out of bed feeling stronger. She needed her clothes. She found her case in his closet and her clothes neatly folded in his bureau, did he expect her to stay forever?

She hurriedly packed her stuff into her case and dressed in a black striped pants suit with a white camisole. She wanted to regain any manner of formality. Her head felt a bit light but she had to muster all her strength since her packing had fairly taken all out of her. She went over to the bathroom and tidied her hair into a ponytail. Her face had shrunk, she had lost some weight, and her clothes were loose about her body. Her makeup made her look decent again and hid the dark circles around her eyes and red blotches in her cheeks. She tidied the bed and descended the stairs. Dmitri was not in the house and since the kitchen door was open, he must be outside. She would call a cab to pick her up.

Outside was a welcome sight. The gardens were immaculate with roses and carnations; there was also a good-sized kitchen garden, with herbs and vegetables in various stages of growth. Dmitri was not in the immediate back yard so she followed a stone path and noticed another cottage; a smaller one but hidden nicely in between some bushes. Who lived there? More mafia men? June thought.

The stone path led to a lake. Dmitri was on the jetty near a boat. He was speaking to two men dressed in black suits. Were they his henchmen? He was talking quickly in Spanish to them. This man was full of surprises, how many languages did he speak?

June decided to return to the house and not disturb the 'mafia'.

This place was indeed a slice of paradise. It was very tranquil and quiet.

She needed a cab or some form of transport to get her out of here. She was about to call a cab when she heard the creak of the boards and turned around. Dmitri's eyes showed that he was shocked by her appearance.

She tried to look confident as he gazed at her scowling. He was obviously displeased to see her standing there dressed and with her bags around her.

"Well, since I'm feeling much better I must get back to my world," she was deliberately avoiding his gaze, " but first I must thank you for all that you have done these past three days I know it was an intrusion but I am totally grateful."

She put some distance between them and walked a bit further into the room. He was just standing there with his hands in his back pockets.

She faced him now "I do not know how I can repay you for your help but "she stretched out her hand, he hesitated before he reached out to take it. However, he stepped forward and pulled her closer to him.

"Stay with me tonight." he said quietly holding her in his arms. She tried to break free,

"I can't." she cried weakly.

"You asked what you can do to repay me... stay tonight." June was distressed. She did not know what to say. He was asking her to stay with him. She looked at him and the expression on his face showed her the passion he had for her. They both knew what would happen if she stayed the night.

"I-" she stuttered

"Just say yes," he whispered against her lips.

" Well," she moaned as he nibbled her lower lip.

"Yes" she released as his lips captured her words into his mouth.

She relaxed in his arms as their kiss deepened, he moulded her to him and she could feel the hard presence of his erection pressed against her stomach. She warmed up all over as she let herself be drawn into the essence of their kiss. He was a skilled kisser, he was passionate yet fierce and she had no doubt how much he wanted her. She had never felt so consumed by such intense passion before.

Did she take a chance and stay or leave and forever regret the one time she had to fulfil her own passionate feelings?

She wrapped her hands around his neck as his hands went under her white camisole. His hands were electric against her skin as she felt a tremor pass through her entire being. She crushed herself closer to him as his hands moved to the undersides of her breasts. His hands were caressing her as he pushed up her bra and let her breasts spring free. She moaned into his mouth as his fingers gently squeezed her nipples. June was mesmerized by the forceful desire coursing through her. She had never been kissed like this, not even by Gary who she thought was the best kisser in high school.

She was floating on a cloud until she felt empty, and slowly realised that Dmitri was no longer kissing her although he was still holding her. She slowly opened her eyes and found him staring at her his hair was mussed and his lips were so full and pink. She tried to regain her standing but he kept her close to him. She could feel the rock of his length against her chest and she stiffened.

"Come with me," he commanded as he led to the living area. She fixed her clothes and followed him silently.

"Dmitri" she said trying to tell him that this was all new territory for her.

"Go rest while I prepare you some dinner, you still look a bit tired."

June was lost in a battle. She had actually agreed to stay a night with him. He pulled her in an embrace and kissed her senseless again. June was now weak from his kisses.

He smiled and said "Go on," sensing her hesitance. She had made her decision. She climbed the stairs anticipating the evening's events. The sun was setting and it cast a golden glow into the house. She took her case to her former room, unsure what to do. She took off her suit and put on her night dress.

She lay on the bed ready to think this through but her eyelids were heavy and closed soon after she snuggled under the covers.

Dmitri checked on June she was not in his room but the one she had been in on the first night. She looked so beautiful and at peace as she slept. He brushed a loose strand off her face and smiled.

June awoke to a soft noise from outside. She sat up and it all came back to her with a heavy lump in her stomach. She knew that it was night and that Dmitri was probably waiting for her downstairs. She was unsure what to do.

She was nervous but excited. She put on a pair of red lace underwear and snuck into Dmitri's room and put on a white shirt of his she found in his closet. She descended the stairs slowly and noticed him in the kitchen. He was humming a popular song along with the artist on the radio. He looked up at her and a smile spread across his face as he took in her outfit.

"Would you like something to drink?" He asked

"Some juice please." She answered sitting on one of the counter top stools.

"You seem very competent in the kitchen." June remarked looking at the pots steaming on the stove and Dmitri expertly cutting some vegetables.

"My mother insisted that her son know how to cook." Dmitri smiled while handing her a glass of orange juice.

"She must be proud."

"She is." Dmitri was not very forthcoming and June presumed in his line of work privacy was important.

"I can't really cook." June admitted. "My mother gave up on me after I exploded the microwave and broke the blender."

They laughed and continued to chat light heartedly about June's kitchen disasters.

They sat to eat a meal of tossed salad, couscous and spetzofai. It was very sumptuous meal because Dmitri was a great cook. Spetzofai is a traditional Greek dish made with sausages, peppers, chillies and onions.

"So what do you do apart from cooking?" She asked quietly, " I mean as a hobby?" June rushed to correct herself not wanting to know anything about his real line of work.

Dmitri laughed before he answered. "I fish, I fly, and I do a lot of outdoor sports like hiking."

"Fly as in a plane?' This man was perfect. He spoke well knew how to cook and had good hobbies. A pity he was a mobster. He had such charm which sucked her in easily.

"Yeah I learned ten years ago, it has a feeling of freedom in it."Dmitri revealed openly as his gaze continued to devour her.

"I always wanted to learn but I never found the time." June took a sip of some wine momentarily looking away from the gaze which captivated her.

"When was the last time you had a vacation?" he asked staring at her, the heat barely contained in his gaze.

"I don't know if a few days to see my sister graduate could be counted as a vacation." Dmitri grabbed her hand and caressed her palm slowly running his fingers in a circular motion in the centre.

"You are in need of some really serious down time... I used to believe that work was the beginning and end all until recently." Dmitri said softly and June almost wrenched her hand from his as her body started to grow warm from his touch.

Dmitri did not elaborate and June was not going to ask. However his brown eyes looked angry for a moment before he held himself in check.

"Is that why you were so angry when I first came here?" she changed the topic.

He smiled, "Well, you did invade my home, well not mine technically but my boss." He leaned forward and said softly "Plus you did catch me rather nude if I remember correctly." she bent her head and blushed using the opportunity to snatch her hand away.

"You were pretty nasty, if I remember correctly," she countered staring back into his twinkling eyes.

It was his turn to smile, "I had just come in after a long and arduous two weeks of tough work. I thought you were an intruder and I guess I was frustrated that you had invaded my space but now," he took her hand again. " I quite like your company June Stapleton."

June shivered from the intense stare he was giving her as he kissed her hand leisurely sucking on her fingertips. June wa a bundle of nerves how could one man create such emotions within her.

Dmitri's answers were too simple but she felt something was missing. She too had her secrets but the sadness he had shown when they had first met was too raw maybe for him to admit. He was recovering from something; she hoped that this time away would heal whatever wounds he was holding.

They finished dinner and tidied up. He led them to the living area where they watched some news and snuggled while being entertained by a sitcom. She knew that tomorrow they would be back to their own worlds but tonight she would savour this experience with Dmitri, at least she would be alive for one night. She snuggled into his chest and hugged him closer almost drifting into sleep as the air became cool.

Dmitri stood up spread a blanket on the floor in front of the fireplace. He knelt on the blanket and beckoned her to him. She moved as in a trance into his open arms. They knelt before each other on the soft rug, their lips joined and the fire exploded within them. The heat escalated to a point of no return. June pulled him to her and they collapsed on the floor with him onto top of her.

He nibbled her ear as she ruffled his hair. His hands were doing magic with her hips as he squeezed her to him. She arched and his hands slipped under her shirt and slowly opened it. He kissed her chest each time he undid a button. Soon, she lay before him exposed in her underwear.

"You are beautiful." He told her as he removed her bra and flung it away. He cupped her breast as he softly moulded them under his hands. June arched her body sizzling from his touch.

"Oh June how I want you so much." Dmitri whispered against her stomach as his hands pulled off her underwear. He continued to kiss her stomach gently with soft butterfly kisses flowing down her thighs. she rubbed her legs together her heat building within her. June was on fire.

Dmitri removed his shirt exposing his solid and firm chest. She stared at his body the ultimate model of perfection as he removed the rest of his clothing. She had already seen him naked but his body was too perfect to not want to see again and again. He stood over her as he took out a condom from his jeans. Dmitri knelt then held her legs and pulled her to him slowly bringing them together. Their joining was slow and sensual and June had never thought she could experience such a subliminal feeling.

Dmitri marvelled at the thought that such a dynamic woman would still be a virgin. She was meant to be his. Later they soaped each other in the shower and ecstasy was repeated.

They made love once more in the early morning when the air as still and quiet. Afterwards they slept fitfully in each other's embrace.

Chapter 6

June awoke feeling tired, a bit sore, but so pleased and so complete that she did not want to move. What she had experienced with Dmitri had not come close to her earlier attempts at lovemaking. She never knew that sex with a person could bring such utter wholeness and contentment. She turned onto her side away from Dmitri's warmth knowing that this was the decisive moment.

The sun had already risen way above the trees; she needed to start her departure. She looked across at her lover... ooh it felt good saying that about the Adonis at her side. He was the perfect lover. She sidled her way to the edge of the bed trying not to disturb his sleep. She crept out of the room not before glancing at him one last time. His lashes fell so tenderly against his cheeks; he was beautiful man and an excellent lover.

She went to her room where she bathed and dressed. She found a telephone book and called a cab but the driver refused to come such a distance to pick her up. Frustrated she flung the phone on the bed, "So much for a clean get away." she murmured to herself. She looked up and noticed Dmitri standing in the doorway. His head was mussed and she remembered running her fingers through it. He had on a pair of jeans but his chest was left exposed and she could clearly see the marks of her fingernails on his sides, she gulped.

"Morning," she offered, "I figured I should make a start."

He leaned against the door jam and shrugged.

"No convincing you to stay."

She closed her eyes, and took a deep breath, if she did not leave now, she did not think she ever would.

"I must leave," she said steadily as if trying to convince herself of her decision. "The night is over."

He straightened and entered the room "If you believe that you must," he was towering in front of her. She nodded unable to speak. He held her head in his hands and lifted her chin.

"Thank you for giving me a special part of you, I enjoyed it too," she almost died then, was he for real?

She smiled as he kissed her but broke it early as he retreated to the door "Let me shower and I'll drop you off in town."

She stood there hugging her self, afraid to speak. If she stayed she knew exactly how hey would spend their days but she had forgotten her life for too long vacation or not she had to move on this diversion was just that a diversion from reality they both had their own lives and she needed to return to hers and he needed his peace and quiet.

Thirty minutes later, they were on their way to town in another of Dmitri's secrets a brand new black truck. It was a Ford Ranger, one of those huge trucks that took the whole road. He drove it as he made love passionately yet fiercely. She glanced at his hands holding the wheel and remembered how he held her last night.

"Stop it!" she cajoled her self.

"What did you say?" he asked.

"Um... nothing" she was too embarrassed at having spoken her thoughts.

They arrived at the town using the road she had discarded on her way. It was a small place with few streets but still modern enough. They had arranged for a local towing company to deliver the truck to the gas station clerk. She thought it would be expensive but the towing man told her that he knew the guy and would do it cheaply.

Dmitri offered to drive her to the nearest airport but another ride with him and they would be making love in the cab of the truck she could barely control her libido on the ride to town. She opted for a train ride instead. They stood on the terminal waiting for the train; the overhead sign was showing that it would arrive in eight minutes. The train would bring her directly to Spakane airport so there would be no hassle after the hour train ride.

"Dmitri," she announced " I do want to thank you for all that you have done and well last night was magical but I'm sure our lives are too separate for us even think that this will go further."

She paused, he was staring at her with his hands folded across his chest and his feet apart, she was intimidated not knowing what he was feeling.

"I do not regret meeting you but I guess if we ever meet gain it will be great to see you again."

She offered her hand and he laughed,

"We will meet again and maybe then we won't be too busy for just one night." she stepped back but he stepped forward and pulled her to him and ravished her with his mouth. They kissed oblivious to the onlookers around them. The train arrived and he put her away from him. She touched her lips which were sore from his lovemaking. She put on her coat, picked up her case, as the conductor put on her carry case. "Bye." she said as she stepped on board the train.

"Adios mi cara" he said as she disappeared. He stood there hands in his pockets thinking.

He remained there until the train pulled away before he returned to his truck, pulled out his mobile and made an important phone call.

June sat in silence. She hoped never to meet Dmitri again, their encounter would be a secret she would cherish all her life. She had never felt like she did in his arms but circumstances have driven them apart. He had a life he needed to escape from while she had one she needed to escape to. Wow what a night! Dmitri had been so skilled so precise. April had spoken highly of sex, losing her virginity at the age of eighteen. She laughed, she had totally forgotten about her family while she was with Dmitri, he consumed her and that was one of the reasons that she needed to escape him.

The train ride was uneventful but it gave her a lot of time to think. Her whole life was centred on making people around her happy and comfortable. She needed to start thinking of her self. If Dmitri had desired her so much as a woman imagine how other men felt. So many guys had been interested in her but she had spurned their interest and consumed herself in her work. Dmitri had shown her to desire herself, and love it. Hey, she was going to do so, stop living for everyone else and start living for herself. Her mobile rang, it was her mother.

"Hi, Mom, what's up?" she said chirpily,

"You're sounding better, how's the recovery going?"

"Great actually, I'm heading home for some more r & r."

"Where are you?" her mother asked

"I'm on a train headed to Spakane Airport." she answered looking at the aforementioned town in the distance.

"Is Dmitri with you?"

"Mom, Dmitri and I well, we need some time apart."

"But you have just started something..." her Mother sounded flustered.

"I know, but things didn't work out as I thought." she said feeling it in her heart.

"Well honey, I do hope you can work things out he seems to be a good man!"

"Well, we'll see." the train had stopped and the passengers were getting off. "Mom, I have to go the rain has arrived and I must disembark, I'll speak to you later, give Dad my love." she spoke quickly as she manoeuvred her way off the train. The air was chilly so she pulled her coat closer to her body. She proceeded to the airport terminal looking forward to her future.

For the first time in her life June felt reckless abandonment. She had two weeks off work and so she did something reckless. Her holiday to the beautiful island of St. Lucia was exceptional. She sunbathed, shopped and went on countless sight seeing trips around this island paradise. At the end of the week she was relaxed and happy.

Dmitri would never know the influence his encounter had caused her to break down the walls she had erected around herself for years. She had kept herself in check trying to follow the rules in being the first born. The realisation that she had the freedom to explore was great. She now had a confidence to move on and to take risks. Maybe she would date more, get a boyfriend whoever said a career woman can't have both.

June walked into the office building refreshed and energized the past two weeks had purged her. She was ready for a whole new approach to her life. The receptionist Debbie greeted her cheerfully as she walked past. Her boss was outside of her office as she approached.

"Welcome back Ms Stapleton," greeted Mr. Hamilton, " You have surely brought new business to this company."

She smiled," Thank you sir, it feels good to be back."

He held the door open for her, as she entered her office. This was once a room in which she had spent more time than her own apartment. It had a heavy desk in the centre and two leather chairs in front. There were two Boston Ferns near the window. On her desk she had a picture of her family. Her office had been filled with basic furniture and sparse.

She put her things down, and sat down, "So sir, how may I help you this morning."

He sat opposite her, "Last week we received a call from the international conglomerate company Breusk Shipping, that is the parent company, but it is made up of several smaller ones. The owner is a Greek tycoon Demetrious Tzarch von Kanaredes who made his wealth from being street smart. He started with one boat and now fifteen years later he owns a hundred times that amount. One of his companies contacted us to prepare a proposal for them."

June barely was listening another rich person wanting to invest and be pampered. She was tired of the same theme.

"So what do they want?" she asked obligatorily.

"They are starting a small retreat complex for pampered executives, a cottage type of resort with individual cabins but with golf courses and the likes. A retreat away from the workplace, really." He stood up and poured himself some coffee that her secretary Wilma had prepared. "They want us to prepare a marketing proposal on the area to set up such a retreat ...etc..."

She breathed in deeply, "Good, how much time do we have?"

"Three weeks." she raised her eyebrows, typical rich folk, expecting the earth to stand still while they are served.

"I'll get started on it right away." she was ready for this challenge.

"I'll get Jay and Minoa on the team since they were excellent the last time."

"As long as you do the ground work, anyone can follow it up." He walked to the door; "Good to have you back, we all missed you." he left on that note.

Things were changing she realised her boss had never been very personal with her, he was not harsh but he had never been so interested in her welfare. Looking back, June realised she had never let anyone get involved in her personal life in the office. This was sure going to change she needed to open up to be freer, to explore and be her own person and that involved leaving the office at normal hours.

She would be a model employee but still take time for herself. She brooded over Dmitri but if she never saw him again she never regretted her encounter with him, she would cherish that experience for a life time. She sighed deeply and pushed her chair closer to the desk, enough rendezvousing time for some serious work. She picked up the phone and dialled an extension number.

"Jay," she spoke into the receiver.

"Hey, you're back, how was the time off?" he asked sounding genuinely interested.

"Great, I have to prove it." she was smiling, it sure felt good be so free.

" Wow, so what's new?"

"Hamilton wants us to work on a new account, a real international one this time, can you make it here in fifteen minutes." she shuffled her papers on her desk. "Find out as much as you can about Breusk Shipping."

"Sure see you soon." he rang off and she dialled her next associate.

Her day had began.

She researched Greek tycoon Demetrious Tzarch von Kanaredes, from all accounts he was a filthy rich billionaire and all from sweat and tears. He was not a regular rich guy but rather a recluse who shunned the limelight and the fast life. He was pretty private individual and rarely ventured to social events although he was very generous and donated heavily to charity namely cancer research since his father had died from it a few years ago. He had one sister and his mother was still alive. Other information about him was very limited, this guy took privacy to a whole another level.

There were very few photographs of him and those that were in print had him blurred or at a distance. He reminded her of Dmitri the same tall stature and dark hair. Kanaredes was Greek whereas Dmitri was Sicilian. What was she thinking, there was no way. The man who had nurtured her back to health lovingly captured her heart and was a member of the mafia was by no means a shipping tycoon.

Chapter 7

The three weeks passed quickly and June was tired, but this was her mission and she completed it. Her mornings were clouded with nausea and outright fatigue by the end of the day; she would have to drag herself home on most days. Her mother recommended that she take some vitamins to replenish her body which was obviously tired and still recovering from her bout of sickness. She would surely do that after her presentation with this new client. June was worried after her bout with hypothermia, she realised that she was not invincible, her body was reacting to years of extensive strain; she needed to take everything easy.

She had been on two dates during the last few weeks. She had let herself explore a new side of dating. Currently she had settled on Gared Thompson, a thirty-four year old accountant. He was pleasant and very jovial. He had a good sense of humour and made her feel at ease. She had met him in the foyer of the office building on several occasions. She had shared an elevator with him twice before he had asked her out.

They had been dating for the past week and a half. Her parents were pleased she was dating; according to her mother, she thought she would never have put her career on the side for her love life. Her sisters on the other hand were shocked and more scandalous, they had nicknamed her "the career" and now they had to swallow their words.

June had dressed exceptionally formal today. She wore a red woven tweed sleeveless dress with a bateau neckline and matching jacket that was the length of the dress. She matched it with nude pumps and a roped pearl necklace.

It was presentation day and at 3:30 pm she and her team were due to make a presentation to this new client. They had completed all work yesterday and this morning would be to tie up some loose ends. She was letting her hair grow, something she rarely did but Dmitri had mentioned that her face was made for long hair. Her hair now brushed her shoulders and already it had softened her face. She had gone to the hair salon the day before and had put in highlights which softened her dark hair. Today however she twisted her hair into a knot and put it in a Japanese style chopstick pin, small wisps of her flowed around her face and completed the effect.

Although her stomach was queasy she had a glow about her. She looked at her reflection and she was blooming, she didn't know why but she was happy and her face always had a flush. Gared had commented that she looked real maternal. June had laughed, she was not ready to have children not until she met her prince. She wanted to meet her real life prince who would sweep her off her feet, she was turning into an utterly hopeless romantic.

She turned way from the mirror and prepared to leave, a sudden wave of nausea hit her. It was getting worse each day. She rushed to the toilet and heaved up the cup of tea she had had for breakfast. She needed to be free of this bug, it was draining her totally.

June arrived at the office to find it buzzing

"What's going on?" she asked her secretary.

"The Greek tycoon is coming to the presentation, Hamilton is all bothered by the fact." June was surprised. She had thought he would be sending a lower minion. It was a good thing she always poured out her best when she worked.

"Wow, I guess the red carpet will be rolled out!" she commented and Wilma smiled. She entered her office and immediately Mr. Hamilton was on the phone.

"Good morning, sir," she greeted.

"Good morning, June, have you heard the news as yet?" he asked

"Yes, the big boss will be over for the presentation." she took off her coat.

"Indeed, ensure that the conference room is set up by midday and have a final run through by eleven."

"Will do sir," she acquiesced as her stomach lurched "I'll get on it right away."

"I know you will ace it, you're one of the best June." he rang off as she headed to the toilet. Her stomach was really acting up today, she was more nervous than she thought. Wilma gave her some antacids but she only sent them back up.

"June, maybe you should go to the nurse." Wilma suggested after her third visit to the toilet.

"I am just anxious about this meeting and need to get through it. I'll be fine." she was adamant but after her fourth visit to the toilet, she knew she needed help from a medical person. She trudged to the company nurse's office on the ground floor and explained her dilemma. The nurse's response shocked her speechless.

"Ms. Stapleton, are you okay?" was she okay? After dropping a bomb like that, she could never be okay again. Her hand went automatically to her stomach. She never thought that she could be pregnant.

Pregnant!

"Do you want to do a test?" the nurse inquired.

"Yes" she stumbled to respond.

Dmitri had used protection every time except in the shower, the wonderful memories of the shower.

She knew the results would be positive before she saw them. She was pregnant and she knew the exact date of conception. June took several minutes to compose herself before she could leave the office, the nurse suggested she visit her doctor soon and gave her some crackers to help stabilised her stomach. She walked in a daze to her office. Wilma was eagerly awaiting her arrival.

"June, are you alright?" she asked kindly

"Yeah, I'm okay, just a passing bug." she lied as she went directly into her office and shut the door. She leaned against it and sank to the floor. She was pregnant with Dmitri's child, the shock was insurmountable. How would she cope? She wasn't ready to be a mother, yet, she wasn't angry. The thought was not repugnant to her, it brought a flush to her skin. She would now have a piece of Dmitri forever, forever she was carrying a baby, hers and Dmitri. He would never know but she would and she would cherish his life inside of her always.

She touched her stomach and smiled. It took the sound of her phone ringing mercilessly to get her off the floor. It was time for the final prep meeting. She was on a high. She was ready for the afternoon meeting. The time drew near and she was spilling over with happiness. Thanks to the nurse's advice, her stomach had decided to give her an ease so she could only eat a light sandwich for as brunch.

June entered the conference room and did another check of the room. Everything was in place. She went over the sitting arrangements. Her boss would seat at one end of the 25-seater table with the Great tycoon on the other. She would be on Hamilton's right side, Jay next to her and Minoa on the boss's left. The time dwindled down to and soon the phone rang to inform them that the team from Breusk Shipping was in the building. June greeted their guests by the door. As each one entered the room they were escorted to their seats by a junior assistant. There were six of them in total.

Mr. Hamilton was escorting the great man himself to the room; they were all standing around the table when Mr. Hamilton entered the room with Demetrious Tzarch von Kanaredes. They each went to their designated positions and June was stunned into paralysis. She sat down dazed. The impeccably dressed tall Greek tycoon was none other than Dmitri, her Dmitri. He regarded her coolly and gave her a warm smile. She was blank, no way, there had to be a mistake. She could not sit comfortably in her chair. Her mind was fuddled as she tried to remember her presentation. She had to compose herself; she took a deep breath and shuffled her papers.

She could do this. She barely heard Mr. Hamilton's preamble speech and looked up from her papers to try to fit into the proceedings but her gaze clashed with Dmitri's who was watching her intently. She could not read his eyes but they were fixed on her which made her even more uncomfortable. She had to do this because now she was angry. He had lied to her about his name that he was everything had been a lie and she hated him for it plus... she was pregnant. What a mess? A day that should have been so memorable was turning into a nightmare. She closed her eyes and stood up as Mr. Hamilton invited her to take over. She blindly went through her presentation. She was mechanical; she remembered what she had to do and did it. She did her best to avoid Dmitri's glances through out the meeting and answered his questions as unemotionally as she could muster.

It all fit why he was so supercilious of her presence and how he contrived to rearrange her life by making one phone call. He was used to his dominating power, when he spoke people scurried to do his bidding. No wonder he felt her disobedience a challenge, he wasn't used to being defied.

At the end of the meeting she hurriedly gathered her papers; she needed to leave the room because she was feeling very claustrophobic by being stared down by Dmitri. He was stifling her. She made excuses to Mr. Hamilton, thanked her associates and dashed out as Dmitri was making his way to their end of the table. The elevator doors were just closing when she saw him exit the room and stare at her in her moment of escape. She rushed to her office; the corridors were basically empty since most of the staff had already left to go home including her secretary. The clock there showed it was a quarter to six.

The meeting had been long and very thorough. She normally stayed to socialise but today she was emotionally overwrought to face Dmitri, she could not, not today, not now. She sank into her chair to breathe before she left the office. She put on her coat, gathered her handbag and briefcase and pulled open the door and run into a solid chest. She knew exactly who she had collided with and her stomach churned. She took a step back and looked up at him. Dmitri's face loomed over her.

"May I come in June?" he asked politely.

"It's late and I have to go home," she said not moving out of the way.

"We can either do this in the corridor or inside your office?" his voice was calm and controlled. The look on his face was serious and he was a man in control who did not back down easily. June was tired and she wanted this whole confrontation to be over, the sooner the better.

June made the choice to step away from the door; the serious look on Dmitri's face was one she had seen before on their first meeting.

He closed the door quietly and stepped further into the room. His imposing presence made her queasy, she wanted to throw up but she couldn't, he could never know that she was pregnant. He would believe that she was just what he first thought another woman trying to capture him in a paternity suit.

She turned away to hide her discomfort from him, but it was too late.

"Is knowing who I am, so disgusting to you?" he inquired grudgingly as she put her stuff on the desk.

"Yes, you lied to me." she accused him openly.

"I did at first because I had no choice, you were a stranger, an invader of my privacy. I had to be careful." he was standing at her desk gazing out of the window.

"Really, you had ample opportunity to tell me the truth after you checked me out." she admonished.

He turned to face her.

"I had to be careful," he repeated.

"This is crap and you know it everything was a lie. I don't know who you are Dmitri the mafia or Demetrious the billionaire!" she flung at him pulling her coat closer to her for some form of comfort. He stared at her for a long time and came to stand in front of her. "My mother called me Dmitri." He touched her cheek lightly and she turned her face and moved away.

"We had something special." he went on.

"To me it was, to you it was just a game with the poor folk."

"Come on June, is knowing who I am so bad?" he was so calm that it grated on her nerves.

"What makes me mad is that you lied to me." June reiterated firmly.

"We all lie June," he was staring at her, "we all have secrets, and sometimes we have to lie to protect our secrets."

"I never did." she screamed losing control, " I was completely honest the entire time and you let me ..., you let me...." she could not voice it. She had surrendered her virginity to him after all these years she had lost it to a man she thought was her prince instead he was a fake.

"We had a great time June it was a beautiful time we shared don't sully it with bad thoughts."

"It is already too late. Now I am repulsed by the whole thought." she was really repulsed because at that moment, she wanted to throw up.

He read the look on her face and his own features clouded up. "We cared about each other June, and now we move on to a new dimension." Was he mad? Had he lost his crackers, did he expect her to just saddle up and forgive him so easily?

"A new what? You want exactly what now from me?" she stared him down.

"I want you.... to be with me, June."

Chapter 8

He did not just say that. After lying to her he expected them to just move on without any thought, all in a day's work she guessed.

"No!" she responded easily.

"I missed you," he stepped closer, "we don't have to end because of who I am."

She moved away from him when he was close she could not think.

The memory of their time together was so raw and vivid in her mind that she fought hard to push them out of her mind.

"I can't, my life here doesn't allow it."

"June," his hands were on her shoulders he pulled her to him and she could feel his desire rock hard against her back. She wanted to just melt into his arms but she could not, she had too much at stake right now. She stepped out of his clutches.

"I have a date," she said turning round to see his reaction. Gared was taking her out to see a musical; he had gotten the tickets last week. She had been excited since she had never been to one before. This musical was a Broadway hit and was continually sold out and since she had always wanted to see one when Gared got some tickets from a client she was overjoyed. "I am going to see the Prairie Tree and I do not want to be late.'

His brows were pulled together in a deep scowl, "Break it!" he commanded.

"I'll be late." she moved to pick up her stuff. "I have my own life Dmitri one which does not include you."

"Ok, you want to make me feel jealous," He came to her and held her face. " It's fine but you know that this thing between us is fuelled by passion." He bent to kiss her and she walked away.

"June you want me and you just felt how much I want you, let's stop all these games and come back to my hotel with me." he was reaching out to her, she sidestepped him again. "Stop pushing me away, don't deny us."

"Is that all I am to you, a lay, a sex doll?" she reproached him as his face contorted in anger. She pushed on realising that he was getting angry with her.

"You know you're not." he was seething, she could clearly see.

"If I leave with you, we both know what will happen but tomorrow, you leave and then what? Huh? You go back to your high tech life and what?" she pressed on feeling really energised by the look of shock and anger on his face. "Every time you're in town you ring me up? Is that how it will go? Hey June care for some sex tonight? Is that how it will be?" she stopped her chest heaving.

"Maybe you get me a nice house in a rich area or something and lavish me with gifts so whenever you call I will be ready to give you all the sex you want?" she continued scathingly.

June had she hit the nail on the head, by his stance it seems the truth being spilled so openly was ugly but he needed to know that she was no easy lay. She turned away from him.

There was utter silence as he stared at her she could see the muscle in his cheek twitching sporadically but his face was devoid of emotion. His hands clenched at his sides repeatedly as he tried to control the urge to throttle her. She was deliberately antagonising him. He got even more furious as he watched her, her eyes goading him on to explode.

She was standing tall as she faced him. Dmitri looked at June. She was unafraid and although she had melted in his arms she was acting as if he did not mean anything to her. Had she really moved on with someone else? Was he too late? He doubted it. She had been untouched until their encounter at his cottage. She would not have moved on so quickly, he was sure. She was just trying to pay him back for not telling her his real identity. He unclenched his hands and stepped toward her. She was his and he was not going to let her slip away this time. Their short association had left him wanting more, much more and he wanted her as his own.

June Stapleton was his and he would have her.

"I need to go home. I am sure we will meet again but only in a business way." she moved to the door. "You may control an empire and had your jolly old laugh making fun of me but once bitten is a far as I go. Never again. I thought the time we had was precious but now looking at you, learning just what kind of man you are, you just disgust me and I hate you for what you did, just remember that!" She stormed out not glancing back. She headed straight to the lift. She only breathed when the doors were closed, this time he had not followed her.

Dmitri let her go. She was a tiger alright and he would her leave this time but he knew that it was just a matter of time before he had her in his arms again. He smiled; let her feel that she had won. Let her come to terms with the truth and then they will move one. June was proving to be just the challenge he needed.

Yes, he wanted to take care of her but as his only woman. However he knew she had more to offer, she was a great business woman and her work was exemplary and he admired that about her. She was the kind of woman he wanted, no needed beside him. He was excited just thinking about how he was going to enjoy taming his tiger woman.

June rushed to her flat and tried to relax but how could she? Dmitri was here in town, in her life..... their companies were on the verge of signing a very lucrative business deal which she was in charge of. How was she going to hide her pregnancy? Would he admonish her if knew? Dmitri would be furious, he guarded his life so well, and he was overly protective of his family? She was not going to be the woman who disturbed his quiet world.

She wanted this child and if she knew Dmitri he would never let her raise this child alone. He would and to take full control that is why she was not going to let him find out about the pregnancy. She didn't know how she was going to execute her plan but she was determined to do it. She had to hide her condition for as long as possible until she was sure what she was going to do.

However tonight she was going out with Gared, he was a sweet guy and soon she would have to tell him the truth but until then she would savour the thought of being with a normal man and not the fantasy of Demetrious Tzarch von Kanaredes. She dressed carefully not wanting to bring any undue glamour to her abdomen. Although she was barely five weeks, she was conscious of it and so she chose a simple red chiffon dress. It was floor length Grecian style dress with a scooped halter neckline with black straps. The back was bare and low. She wore a pair of black Louboutins and a clutch purse. She had bought this dress along with six others after her shopping spree to rejuvenate her wardrobe. It made her torso look longer and lengthened her height. She swept her hair in a messy bun to finish off her look.

Gared was impressed by her appearance. He was blown away by her.

"You look gorgeous!" he said kissing her on the cheek.

"Thank you." she answered as he put on her coat.

"You look pretty dashing yourself," He was dressed in a tuxedo which enhanced his physique and made his blond hair look golden. Gared had a great sense of humour as he bowed to her.

"Glad to please you oh pretty lady." He offered her his arm and they laughed as he helped her into his black Audi Q7 E tron SUV. The conversation to the Royal Theatre was light and airy. Gared was a great conversationalist, for an accountant he wasn't stuffy or outdated but laid back and relaxed.

There were a lot of people in attendance tonight. Everyone was decked out in their most formal wear. Gared escorted her inside, she felt like a princess with her dashing knight beside her. It was unfortunate she had met Dmitri first and that she was pregnant because Gared was a real great guy. The first half was magical. The performers were excellent. They sang, danced, and moved so gracefully and intelligently on stage that she had to wink to ensure that she was actually watching a play and not involved in a fantasy.

The resounding applause at the interval revealed that everyone in attendance was just as appreciative as she was. Gared left her to get some refreshments. She had used the toilet was busily viewing the people milling around her. They were from the echelons of society. The dresses were expensive and all designer labelled and the hairstyles were all coifed and styled to perfection.

She turned around and found her self being stared down by none other than Dmitri, he too was formally dressed in a tux that must have been tailored for him. It fit him splendidly. He was standing there scowling at her but looking exceptionally handsome. She had not wanted to be reminded of him, after walking out on him she was determined to keep him out of her head.

It was a struggle but now seeing him here, it was no use. He made no move to approach her so she simply turned away. He had been conversing with two older gentlemen. He had been staring at her coolly; she took a deep breath, and promised herself that he was not going to spoil her night.

Gared came back shortly and handed her some sparkling water. She was grateful for the distraction. They continued to mingle with the crowd, since some of them were clients of Gared's they welcomed him warmly. June tried her best to forget Dmitri's presence but she could feel him staring at her as she moved around with the crowd. When Gared saw an executive from his company, he guided her to have a chat with him. He had his hand lightly around her waist as they walked toward his colleague. He introduced her and they began a short conversation.

Mr. and Mrs. Wilkins were probably in their fifties and were easy to get along with. Mr. Wilkins worked as a Chief Financial Officer at Gared's company and was commenting on the artistic qualities of the musical. June sipped her drink and chatted with his wife while the men switched the talk to work.

"Mr. Wilkins, pleased to see you again." came a voice which gave June chills.

"Mr. Kanaredes, always a pleasure," Dmitri was shaking hands with Mr. Wilkins looking so sure of himself. What was he doing here? Why couldn't he leave her alone? She stared at him coldly as he wormed his way into their small clique.

"Mrs. Wilkins you look extremely lovely tonight." Mrs. Wilkins was actually blushing. Ooh she wanted to puke.

Mr. Wilkins turned towards them and introduced Gared and herself. Dmitri squeezed her hand a little strongly that she wanted to kick him. She gave him a plastic smile as Mr. Wilkins started to roll off Dmitri's great accomplishments. She rolled her eyes and he glared at her when she did so.

"Ms. Stapleton and I are already intimately acquainted." Dmitri uttered his voice sensual as he spoke.....what was he trying to do? She choked on her drink. Gared was attentive and patted her back,

"Are you okay?" Gared asked her, June's face was red from embarrassment for causing a scene thanks to the lout Dmitri who was glaring at her with a smirk on his face.

"I am fine, I just drank too fast, sorry." She apologised gaining her composure. Gared fussed over her a bit longer than was necessary.

"Are you really okay Ms Stapleton?" Dmitri inquired smugly still basking in his victory but a little perturbed by Gared's over attention.

"I'm fine Mr. Kanaredes." She gave him a stiff smile.

"So Mr. Kanaredes are you acquainted with Miss Stapleton here?" asked Mr. Wilkins looking curiously at them.

"Yes, I have just started on a new venture with Global, I will be seeing a lot of Ms. Stapleton over the next few months." Dmitri drawled. "She is an integral part of the project and we will be working very closely together."

All eyes were now on her. June tried not to meet anyone's eyes. Dmitri's words appeared normal but the underlying meanings were not lost on her.

"Yes, we are so grateful to be dealing with such an international corporation." She smiled sweetly as she supported his statement.

"You chose well Kanaredes, as always, Global is one of the best companies that deal with business promotion and management in fact we do a lot of business transactions with them." Mr. Wilkins added and June smiled, she had cleverly diverted the innuendo Dmitri had tried to insert by his statement.

"So what did you think of the evening so far?" Mr. Wilkins asked moving away from business talk. June was not interested and signed off the conversation. She leaned back and Gared tightened his hand around her waist. She noticed Dmitri's eyes darken so she snuggled closer to Gared. She whispered to Gared that she wanted to excuse herself. Dmitri's eyes were trained on them.

"You must excuse me, but it was a real pleasure meeting all of you." she said as she left the group. Gared held her fingers and kissed them, she gave him her most dashing smile as she moved away.

She glanced in Dmitri's direction his face showed that he was none too pleased. She was happy, did he think she was only his? She went to the ladies room and composed herself. Dmitri was making her do strange things. Blah! She screamed mentally. On her return the intermission was over so they entered the theatre immediately. She did not see Dmitri for the rest of the evening although she knew he was around and probably throwing daggers her way with his eyes. She totally encouraged Gared's flirtations hoping that he would get the message and bugger off. It was not difficult since she enjoyed his company so she just let herself enjoy the evening. Let Dmitri stew on this!

Gared escorted her home and she let him kiss her at her door. He was a good kisser and he left with longing. However she could not enter into a sexual relationship with him. She would have to tell him about her pregnancy soon because she did not want to keep leading him on. He was too nice of a guy to be bogged down by her and her situation. She collapsed against her door; Gared did not bring out any passion in her and she was furious.

She wanted to hurl something at Dmitri, he had spoiled her for other men. How she wanted to hurt him for what he did.

She took off her shoes and drank a glass of water. She undressed slowly and prepared for bed. She decided to put on a light pyjama shirt because she was feeling a bit warm. It was almost midnight but she didn't feel sleepy, she was wound too tight with the events of the day bounce in her head. She flopped onto her bed and started to read a novel.

The phone rang piercing the quiet night, who could be calling her so late? She picked up the phone it was an unknown number,

"Hello?" she said cautiously.

"Good you're awake, open the door!" Dmitri's voice invaded her senses.

"What!" she responded to his command.

"I am standing outside, open the door!" he commanded.

Chapter 9

"It is late, go back to your hotel." she was adamant.

"June open the door we need to discuss things." Dmitri prodded.

"It is late, I have to work tomorrow if you need to discuss anything, call during normal office hours." with that she ended the call.

Soon after, she heard her doorbell in conjunction with loud pounding on her front door. The guy was not going to give up. She lived in a quiet apartment building and loud noises were never heard so late. Dmitri was not letting up. She trudged down her short flight of stairs and flew open the door. He stumbled forward, she wanted to throttle him. He was still dressed in his tux but his bow tie was loose and he had a long black coat over it. He righted himself and walked in. He removed his coat placed it on the back of her sofa and stood there waiting for her to close the door. She did but very slowly.

"Say it quickly so that you can leave." she stood by the closed door defiantly with her arms folded in front of her.

"I will not stand insolence from you." he spoke with a look of determination on his face.

She raised her eyebrows uninterestedly.

"Have you slept with Thompson?" he asked pointedly.

"That is none of your business." she replied, she walked up the three steps to the kitchen area and put on the kettle. He was right behind her, she mistakenly turned around ill judging how near he was. He now put an arm on either side of her, pinning her to the counter.

"I asked you a question now answer me!" Dmitri insisted looking down at her intensely.

"We said goodbye, I never thought I would see you again." She reminded him.

"June, it was never goodbye for me, I knew I wanted you, I waited for the right moment for us to meet again." Dmitri admitted.

"Why didn't you tell me?" she asked feeling a bit overwhelmed by his closeness. "Why did you let me believe it was goodbye?"

"I wanted you to want me for who I am and not what I have." Dmitri informed her, his voice sounding sultry and sexy as he whispered in her ear.

June was annoyed by what he was doing to her body. She was feeling her blood heat up, "I accepted you for the man I met in the cottage on a horrible rainy night. At first you made me want to throttle you but later you showed me how wonderful a man could be and I bore my soul to you Dmitri."

He stepped back and run his hand through his hair. He stared at her deeply. His eyes looked like he was regretful.

"I was in complex negotiations selling one of my companies, I had to be careful." she shook her head, he was giving too many excuses. "I never expected to find you June. I was not looking for a relationship or even an encounter with a woman but you stepped into my life and I knew I wanted you."

He bowed his head and shrugged like he was tired. She wanted to put her arms around him but stilled herself. She needed to see if he was being genuine.

"Be honest you didn't trust me and now it is too late!" he looked into her eyes quickly trying to ascertain if her words were true. Dmitri approached her. He needed the truth.

"Is he your lover now?" he was too close. She couldn't breathe. He held her shoulders, and stared at her, she bent her head and flinched from his touch.

"He is, isn't he? Is that why you no longer want me?" he stepped back abruptly releasing her. He run his hand through his hair again.

"So that's it then, you've moved on?" he was staring at her like a dejected man. June had not uttered a word, she was too shocked to do so. Let him think that Gared was her lover, serves him right for lying to her.

"Yes, I have moved on." she said softly remembering his earlier words that sometimes we need to lie to hide our secrets. She raised her head and the anguish she saw on his face wrenched at her heart. She wanted to take back her words for a moment but she stopped her mouth from opening. She was still in turmoil about her pregnancy. She did not know how to tell him.

"You moved on quickly, I thought...." he stopped himself and turned away from her.

"You thought wrong, when we parted to me it was over. I never thought I would see you again." she repeated not making sense of his reaction. "So to answer your question, yes I have moved on."

He was leaning against the cupboard with his hands in his pocket. He seemed to have aged ten years as he listened to her. His shoulders were now drooping and his eyes were cloudy.

The kettle tinged off and she attended to it turning her back on him. She tried to speak as normally as possible to maintain her farce.

"Do you want a cup of tea or coffee?" She offered opening her cupboard to take out two teacups.

She heard shuffling behind her as he said, "No thank you, I would rather a stiff drink instead."

She turned around and found him looking at her strangely. She could not decipher the look he had on his face but he appeared to be calculating in his head.

"I want you June because you are mine. No other man deserves you." He pulled her into an embrace and turned her around.

June looked up at him and he kissed her before she could speak. The kiss was firm and hungry. It was one of dominance and possession. She did not want to respond but her body had its own ideas. She released her tension and gave in to him. He put his hand under her shirt and caressed her body. Tingles exploded within her as he hauled her onto the counter. She wound her arms around his neck as he deepened the kiss. His hands moved to her breast as he pushed up her shirt. He was now kissing her neck as she moaned.

This feeling was so good. Being in Dmitri's arms again was heavenly. June wrapped her legs around him as she pulled him closer. She pushed his jacket off and pulled his shirt from his trousers as her fingers fumbled to open his shirt.

"You are mine." He whispered as his mouth captured hers again.

Her mobile beeped to signal an incoming message. This made June stop and push Dmitri away. He was looking at her hungrily there was so much smouldering passion on his face. His hair was messy but he looked so alluring.

"Ignore it June." He said as he dipped his head to her breast.

"I should answer it."June said as she screamed in pleasure as Dmitri moulded her breasts using his teeth nip at the sensitive buds. She was losing herself in his touch but the continuous shrill of her phone gave her some strength to push him away and get off the counter.

June tried to breathe as her body was so much on fire. Her nerve endings were all frayed and zapping furiously through her system.

She rushed to get her phone which was on the sofa. She looked at the caller name flashing on the screen.

It was Gared. She paused for a moment. Her hand not reaching out quickly enough. Guilt replacing the burning desire that had been burning in her veins seconds before.

The phone had stopped ringing by the time she eventually picked it up instead a message now popped up from Gared:

You must be asleep but I just wanted to wish you sweet dreams. I had a great time tonight speak to you tomorrow.

This was like cold water on her. She had to stop this with Dmitri.

She had Gared now.

She turned around to find a shirtless Dmitri walking toward her. The look in his eyes spelled the heat her body had been feeling.

She scooted away from him and held out her hands to keep him back.

"This needs to stop okay. I can't do this to Gared." She pleaded. " I can't do this with you."

"Come on June your response just now shows you still want me, he is not the man for you... I am!" Dmitri stated forcefully not moving away from her.

June ran to the other side of the room.

"Please Dmitri, stop, I really can't do this." She pleaded. "How can I work with you and sleep with you at the same time. Everyone at the office will know and my career will be over."

Dmitri captured her and held her in his arms.

"I never mix business with pleasure my love." He kissed her forehead. "End it with Thompson tomorrow and we take it from there."

He kissed her again "See you later Ms Stapleton." his voice was raspy and filled with raw emotion.

June wanted to run to him and beg him to stay but her legs were too weak. She watched him put on his shirt as he mind contemplated ripping the garment form his hands. However, a lot of restraint was felt as she turned her back to hold herself away from him.

"Good bye Dmitri." she said softly as he opened the door and left.

June sank to the floor, her body was wired up with lust but her mind was filled with remorse.

June cried herself to sleep that night. The next morning her eyes were puffy and red. To make matters worse her stomach had not eased its wrenching. She had an appointment with the doctor who gave her a list of things she could do to alleviate the morning sickness. She got vitamins and several leaflets on pregnancy and books she could read to help her cope with her new status. Overall she was okay and if she continued to follow her regimen she should have a healthy baby in a little more than seven months.

She paused outside the doctor's office to stare at a young couple, the woman was probably about eight months pregnant and her husband was diligently helping her to get out of the vehicle. They kissed and they proceeded towards her. She fiddled with her bag as they greeted her when they passed. She was filled with emotion, her eyes welled with tears. She could share this with Dmitri, they should have this loving togetherness. She knew that it was going to be tough, just raising a baby was hard work.

Dmitri needed to know about this child but was he ready to be a father?

She decided that she had to keep her pregnancy secret until she made up her mind when to tell Dmitri. He was a billionaire and she knew she had to be spot on when she delivered the news. She did not want him to think that she wanted to entrap him nor believe that she was after his money.

She proceeded to her vehicle, the next couple of months were going to be rough; but she had to tell her family. Well it was her bed and she had to lie in it. The couple had really affected her. She was yearning for such comfort from a man well actually a certain Greek billionaire.

June did not feel like going back to work so soon so she changed direction, while she was driving June began to wonder... what if?

If only Dmitri was a normal guy and not some billionaire.

If only she had met Gared first, he was just so comfortable to be with.

If only she did not want to ravish Dmitri everytime she saw him.

If only she was sexually attracted to Gared but she wasn't.

There were too many "if onlys" in her life.

She drove to a baby store and started browsing the shelves. All the stuff was so cute and adorable. She had not even thought if she wanted a girl or a boy...in fact it didn't matter, she would be happy with her bundle of joy. Hers and Dmitri's. She was going to cherish this child, this reminder of her liberation, the product of one night filled with passion and release with a man who had been plaguing her thoughts since they first met that rainy night.

June was so confused. She had always been so independent and strong. She had been self sufficient. She had never wanted to rely on a man. She made her own happiness. Now Dmitri had stepped into her life and changed everything. She did not want to lose her independence. She had to regain control. The man was making her lose herself. She had not remained a virgin at her age by chance it had totally been by choice. However she had willingly lost it after meeting Dmitri for a few short days. The man had made such a strong impact. She touched her belly. He had made life changing impact and the result would be a child. Flesh and blood.

She picked up a small pair of booties; they were brilliant white with white lace and ribbon. She put it back in the tray but on second thought she decided to by it. She continued to go through stuff and realised that baby stuff was just so adorable. She had never been close to children partly because none of her friends had any. Or those who did weren't close to her. By the time she left the cashier she had purchased a few pairs of booties, several crochet jumpers, onesies, vests, coats, caps, bibs and blankets. Well at least she had a start. She placed the six bags into her car and smiled. Baby shopping had elevated her mood.

She breezed into the office feeling on top of the world, Wilma was pleased to see her back to her old self. However her morning started to crumble as soon as she was summoned to Mr. Hamilton's office.

His door was open so she entered. She found Dmitri and his personal assistant Franco Mendez already in audience. She greeted everyone and took a seat. She did not glance at him but busied herself with her skirt.

"Good, everyone's here." Mr. Hamilton began, "June, you remember Mr Kanaredes. June barely glanced at Dmitri just nodding her head in his direction. "We have been discussing the new marketing campaign and Mr. Kanaredes would like you to have a more in depth view of the proposal by visiting the business in question."

June sat there shell shocked, he wanted her to do what!? She raised her head and their glances clashed; hers with disbelief and his with triumph. What was he up to she thought?

"Sir, I do not know what to say," she stumbled out and saw Dmitri smile, the jerk had something up his sleeve, she was going to play the game until she found out what it was.

"Great, you have to fly to Sicily, to the property in question to have a better view of the operations, Mr Kanaredes' team will give you a better picture of the development while you are there. You should be there for a few weeks or until you finish the proposal, a month to the most. We thought it would be better if you did this one hands on."

"We?" June thought it was more "He." Dmitri wanted her to come to Sicily, he was forcing her hand, if she went over there she would have no choice but to be on his turf and acquiesce to him plus Gared would not be in the picture. If she had to keep the pregnancy away from him she could not do this. She was stuck, the deal was a splendid one, with so many perks, but it had so many consequences. She was truly stuck.

"The details are all here in this." stated Franco handing her a large brown portfolio. She took it hesitantly.

"I need to go over this," she said trying to buy time.

"Good, so you take the rest of the day to pack, you will be leaving tomorrow morning with Mr. Kanaredes on his plane." June was truly angry now the man was manipulating her. Did he want her so bad or was he just a man who wanted control? She shakily fixed the portfolio on her lap.

"Sir, I don't want to be rude but I can't go." June said firmly trying to stop this railroading of her life.

"What? Ms Stapleton you are in charge of this project of course Jay will accompany you but you need to lead this from the front." Mr Hamilton was a bit confused and the look he was giving her was deadly.

"I know that sir but it's just so sudden, what about my other projects, The Kramer project is due in two weeks and the Salmer opening is next month. I can't abandon my other work like this." Dmitri was glaring at her with a self-satisfied smile. The jerk was sure looking very pleased with himself.

"I have reassigned your other cases. Your only project is this one and you will co-operate fully with Mr Kanaredes."

"Okay sure, thank you sir." She had nothing else to object to.

Up to this point Dmitri had said nothing, the casual way he was leaning in the chair spoke volumes to her, and he was like a cat that had eaten the canary. She could not glare at him because of the positions in which they were seated. He had a better angle and was using it to give her all these victory looks. She wanted to strangle him. How was she going to escape this? She loved her job but she wasn't going to quit but how was she going to hide her pregnancy when they would be in such close quarters.

"That is it then, thank you gentlemen and thank you June." The men stood up and June was in a daze.

Her only hope was that she would not be showing until she was about four months along. She stood up shakily, holding the portfolio as a life line. She wanted to escape from this nightmare, she slowly turned around to leave, but the following words halted her exit,

"May I have a few words with Ms Stapleton alone?" Dmitri asked softly.

Chapter 10

She wanted to scream but just held back quietly. June led him to her office on the next floor. They did not speak in the lift and she nervously walked quickly to her office. She smiled at a stunned Wilma. She rushed to her desk and put the portfolio down. She had her back to Dmitri. The click of the door was like a nail in her coffin.

"I want to see your face June," he commanded softly.

She refused to turn she was so angry she wanted to cry.

"I thought it was polite to face a person when they are speaking to you." He continued saucily.

She still refused to face him fighting back nausea and tears. This pregnancy was making her so emotional and right now Dmitri was not helping her. The smugness of his voice just made her more nauseous and sick. She was struggling to compose her self when she felt his hand on her arm forcing her to face him. He used his other hand to lift her chin to face him. The look he saw on her face brought him to a halt because his mouth closed when he looked at her. Instead of continuing to berate her, he guided her to a chair and put her to sit down.

He then got her a glass of water. He cajoled her to drink it. June was in shock she barely remembered what he was doing, her mind was blank.

"Now breathe, you're having a bit of a panic attack." She could barely hear his voice it seemed so far away.

"I said to breathe, June!" He was losing her, "Come on breathe."

She could not obey his command because her body was getting sleepy she needed to close her eyes for a few minutes until her head felt better. Yes, just a few minutes, and she would be fine. Dmitri was speaking to her his voice filled with urgency but she could not make out the words as her mind drifted away and her body let the faint overcome it.

When she re-opened her eyes, she could see white ceiling and Dmitri at her side. She tried to sit up but Dmitri pushed her down,

"Don't force yourself." He looked so concerned.

"Where am I?" she asked sensing that she was no longer at the office.

"The hospital, I brought you in after you fainted." Dmitri gave her a tight hug, " Oh June you had me so worried when you fell."

June was touched he sounded genuinely concerned. A doctor walked in and Dmitri slowly released her.

"Ms. Stapleton, good to see you awake. I am Dr. Wright. " The doctor looked at the chart he was holding in his hands and June panicked she could not let Dmitri find out about the pregnancy.

"Doctor I am fine, I just want to leave now." She said trying to get out of bed. Dmitri held her back.

"June we need to know why you fainted." She looked at Dmitri before looking at the doctor again.

"Dr Wright, I know what is wrong and I would prefer if we didn't discuss this right now or in front of him." She looked pointedly at the man standing beside her.

Dmitri appeared confused, "June if you are sick I need to know about it." He spoke firmly then looked at the doctor, "Go on."

The doctor could sense the tension and appeared to debate what to do as he looked back and forth between June and Dmitri.

"Well, um," the doctor started again before glancing at his clipboard again and cleared his throat. "Ms Stapleton, you..." the doctor stopped as Dmitri's phone interrupted him.

Dmitri took the phone out of his jacket pocket and looked at the caller before saying, "I really need to take this call but don't say anything until I get back." He warned before getting out of the room.

"Dr Wright, " June said softly, "I'm pregnant and I know fainting can be common in the first trimester."

The doctor shook his head in agreement, " That is true Ms Stapleton but your HB levels are also low, you need to take more iron as the little you have are being sourced to your baby. I have written you a prescription for some tablets."

June agreed, "I will definitely do so. Can I leave now?" she asked trying to get out of bed before Dmitri gets back.

"Your blood pressure was also a bit high, are you stressed about anything?"

June smiled, " You've met my stress already, he just walked out of that door."

Dr Wright smiled, "Ms Stapleton, consistent high blood pressure is dangerous to both you and the baby. You need complete rest and to be stress free."

"Can you give me prescription to get rid of him too?" she asked cheekily.

They both laughed at her joke.

" I am scheduled to fly to Sicily tomorrow." June continued seriously.

" I would advise you not to as your body appears to need complete rest for the next few days. It would be better if you remained in bed for at least two days then see your GP." He looked at his clipboard, "Have you been sick recently, as in a major illness?"

" Umm, I had a mild case of hypothermia and fever around five weeks ago." she responded.

" That explains the presence of antibiotics in your blood stream, well I would hope you take it easy for a few days and see your GP regularly just to make sure."

" Thanks doctor but could you not tell Dmitri about the baby, I haven't told him yet and he is a bit over protective."

Dr Wright smiled, "I understand but no travelling and complete rest or the next few days."

Dmitri walked in while the doctor was speaking, " June are you okay?" he turned to the doctor, " She can't travel?"

"I would advise her to rest completely as her body appears to be a bit weak at the moment, I recommend bed rest for a few days, no stress as her blood pressure is a bit high and she can see the GP in a few days for a check-up."

"Thank you Dr Wright," she said, "Can I get dressed now?"

"Sure you are discharged." The doctor turned to leave, " I will leave your paperwork at the nursing desk."

Dmitri went to him and asked again, "She is okay right, health wise?"

"Yes, she just needs to rebuild her system and rest." With that the doctor left the room.

Dmitri noticed that June was in the en suite. He had to be proactive, pressuring her to be with him was not the way. He needed to change his approach.

"If you ask me how I am feeling one more time I swear Franco will be writing your obituary!" June was exasperated, for the last two days Dmitri had practically moved into her two bedroom flat.

Her once sedate living room was now his "office". His PA had moved his clothes into her spare room and he had a cook and a maid. Yes a cook making them meals throughout the day and a maid ensuring that the place was clean. Her home was no longer hers and she was stuck in her room, in bed.

Dmitri shared a bed with her for the past two nights when he was not on the phone or conference calling. He had not pressured her once for sex. He only cradled her in his arms as they slept and gave her light kisses on her forehead. Just being near him had her libido in shambles, she wanted to tear off his clothes and have unbridled sex with him but he was being a gentleman. It was probably for the best as she was still unsure whether to tell him about the pregnancy or not.

"Okay June, I will leave you alone for now," he kissed her forehead.

"Now eat your food and I will check on you later, I need to video conference with my office in Thailand."

June watched him leave her room. She looked at the food on the table beside her. It smelled delicious and no doubt it was but one taste of the soft mash potato had her rushing to the bathroom to throw up. She tried to ensure that Dmitri did not see her vomiting too often or else he would suspect something. She ate the crackers she had asked the cook to get her.

Mr Hamilton had been understanding, although a bit confused about her time off coinciding with Dmitri postponing the trip to Sicily until next week. Somehow Jay had been elected to go in her place and would be leaving next week. Mr Hamilton sounded suspicious on the phone but June had pretended that she was unaware of Dmitri's plans.

June was awakened by loud noises coming from the living area.

She put on her robe and glanced at the clock it was six pm. She came out to see Dmitri and Franco as well as her parents talking.

"Mom? Dad?" she said surprised.

"Oh honey," her mother rushed to her and gave her a big hug. "Are you alright? Why did you not tell us you were sick?" Her mom was petite and comely, June was a replica of her except for her height.

"Mom, I'm okay now."

Her dad came over and she hugged him as well, He was a tall man and his silvery grey hair made him look dashing with his pronounced dimple in his chin.

"My little girl, what's the matter?"

"I was just tired a bit, I'm fine in fact I am back to work tomorrow."

"No you are not." Dmitri said firmly.

"The doctor said two days rest and today is day two, so tomorrow is back to work." She countered.

"I forbid it. You need more time to recuperate, I already got you time off for the rest of the week."

June was furious who was he to dictate her life.

"Sorry to burst your self appointed dictator bubble but you cannot tell me what to do!" Dmitri came to her and held her shoulders.

"I think you fainting from too much stress shows that you need someone else to tell you what to do."

She shook his hands off her. " What? If anyone will dictate my life it certainly will not be you!"

"June stop being obstinate."

She laughed, " Obstinate? Ha! Who has practically come into my flat and taken it over. I never invited you in the first place!"

"You need to calm down June, you are getting riled up unnecessarily." Dmitri spoke softly like a father to his child.

June got even angrier.

"Don't talk down to me!"

"June get back in bed and rest, you getting yourself angry for no reason."

"You are not my boss go tell Franco what to do!" Dmitri then picked her up and took her to the bedroom.

She was fighting him every step of the way. He laid her on the bed and put her under the covers. June tried to wriggle out but the man was like a cage. He held her firmly in place. She was getting really tired of this.

"Unhand me you bully!" she screamed in frustration.

"Stop moving and behave!" he was looking at her angrily "Why don't you just do what I say and stop being insolent!"

June bit him on the forearm.

"Ouch!" he moaned as her teeth sunk in and stayed there.

"Um excuse me but Mr Kanaredes, you need to respond to the inquiry from Thailand in the next five minutes." Franco's voice came in smoothly and made them realise that they were not alone.

Her parents were staring at them in amusement as well as Franco who was hiding a smile.

Dmitri released her and stood up, "Fine, I'll be right there."

He looked at his right forearm which showcased June's teeth impression. Thankfully she had not pierced his skin. He turned to look at Franco and followed him out the door.

He stopped near her parents and said, "Sorry about that but she needs complete rest."

Her mother patted Dmitri's back, "We know she can be headstrong, go on do your work and thanks for caring."

June folded her arms across her chest and stared at the ceiling.

"June Stapleton, how could you?" her mother admonished as soon as Dmitri had closed the bedroom door.

"He cares about you and all you do is be troublesome. I would never have thought you could be so unruly."

"Mom," she pouted now she was being told off because of Dmitri. All of a sudden she felt emotional and tears started to fall. She went into a full crying binge. She hated her pregnancy hormones!

Her dad hugged her until she stopped crying.

"Oh my little girl, hush no need to to be scared." he patted her back lovingly.

When she was done her mother gave her a tissue and looked at her pointedly and asked, "Are you pregnant?"

Chapter 11

This chapter is dedicated to the lorainesanganoo, orchissa and fiery-whirlpool1 for being my first commenters...thanks it means alot!

June was not enjoying dinner. They were seated around her four piece dining set. Dmitri had asked the chef to create a meal worthy of a five star restaurant. The food was exquisite and June was doing her best to keep it all down. She had eaten some crackers beforehand and had stuck to lightly spiced food which encompassed mainly salad and vegetables on her plate. At least she would not be throwing up. She glanced at her mother who was chatting animatedly to Dmitri about his childhood. Her Dad was also very involved. June was nervous. The conversation in her bedroom earlier had been tense.

"June are you pregnant?" her mother asked pointedly.

June was rendered speechless.

She looked at her mother then her father and then bowed her head.

"You better not lie to me young lady." Her mother admonished.

"Yes." She whispered almost wishing her mother's intuition was not as strong as it was.

"Look at me June." She looked at her mother. "Is it Dmitri's?"

She nodded.

"So? I thought you said the two of you broke up and it was not serious?" her dad asked.

"Well, it wasn't but ...." June was stumbling she wished she was not having this conversation with her parents.

"Come on, what happened and why is he working from your home? Doesn't he have an office?" her mother was shooting questions at her like a bullet.

"He does have an office but he chose to use my place since I fainted at work and he wanted to be near me." June was bunching up the sheets around nervously since her she felt like a criminal being interrogated by the police.

June explained the situation to her parents and told them that she had just found out about the pregnancy and that she and Dmitri were not really 'back together' and that he did not know about the pregnancy as yet. She told them that he was a billionaire and also a client and that it was very complicated. She also told them that she needed more time to organise her thoughts and hoped that they would support her.

Dmitri had invited them to dinner and they had accepted eagerly wanting to know more about this man who was supposedly rich and who had fathered their unborn grandchild.

June looked and listened, her parents and Dmitri were getting on quite well. Her parents were open minded and had welcomed Dmitri in her life, she knew that they were accessing him and from the questions they were asking. Her dad was more cautious but her mom was a no holds barred kind of person.

"June, do you want to rest now?" June was brought back from her reverie by Dmitri's question. She looked at the three pairs of eyes staring at her in anticipation of her answer.

"No, I'm fine. Would anyone like a cup of tea or coffee?" she asked standing up.

"June sit down." Dmitri commanded. "Let the chef prepare the drinks."

It riled June every time he told her what to do. It was his domineering tone of voice which screamed 'Do as I say!' which irked her the most.

"I'm not an invalid plus this is my home." She stated firmly before going to prepare the drinks.

He mom loved herbal tea and her dad just loved regular tea. Since Dmitri was Greek she guessed Dmitri drank strong black coffee. Greeks are famous for their strong taste in coffee. She made herself some chamomile tea as well as her Mom; it was gentle and would help relax her nerves.

She handed everyone their drinks.

"Thanks dear." her Dad said.

"Smells lovely June," her mom commented.

Dmitri looked at his cup and then her before taking a sip. He put the cup down and winked at her.

"Mmm perfect June, thanks."

She tried not to blush guessing he liked it.

"So June we expect you at the barbecue this Saturday, " Her mother said and turned to Dmitri, " You are invited as well Dmitri, it will be at my sister's place, it's a family event we hold every year. I would love you to meet the rest of the family."

June was horrified, "Mom, Dmitri is a very busy man he will not have time to come to Aunt Celia's barbecue."

"Of course I will there Mrs Stapleton, I would be honoured to meet your family, June has told me very little about them." Dmitri's eyes were twinkling with mischief and June wanted to scream.

"Oh that will be just fabulous!" her mother beamed.

June was on edge by the time her parents left her flat. Her dad had gotten Dmitri to volunteer to play on his football team for the Barbecue. The men played competitive six a side football every year. Her Dad and his brother, Uncle Wyatt were the two captains and they were brutal. Each brother tried to win by any means necessary.

June had showered and was ready for bed. She had avoided Dmitri ever since her parents had left. He had been on the phone rattling off in Greek or Italian or one of the million languages he appeared to be fluent in.

She chose her outfit for work the next day and secretly organised her bag. She was determined to go to work the next day in spite of her jailer's demands.

June was nervous if Dmitri held her tonight she would definitely have sex with him. She needed a plan. She paced her bedroom floor but nothing came to her. She peeked out at the living area and noticed that he was now on his laptop but still chatting away on his phone. Does the man ever rest? She thought she was a workaholic but Dmitri took the gold medal.

June had a great idea. She locked her bedroom door and turned off the lights. She got into bed and welcomed sleep. She was a bit tired so she drifted quickly. She was suddenly awakened by loud pounding. She sat up in bed quickly feeling a bit disoriented.

"June open this door!" Dmitri was shouting.

June then remembered she had locked her door. She checked the bedside clock, it was 1 am.

She crawled back under the covers hoping he would give up

"June I know you can hear me now open up before I break down this door." Dmitri was bellowing and pounding.

"June this is ridiculous now open this door NOW!"

June pretended to sleep and tried not to laugh at the situation. She slowly crept to the bathroom because she needed to urinate and hoped his pounding would mask the flushing toilet.

"I am not stopping until you open this door!" Dmitri was saying.

June mimicked him "Open this door!" and almost let out a giggle. There was a calm and Dmitri appeared to have given up. June was closing the bathroom door when her bedroom door was forced open and slammed against the wall. She stood there in mid stride as Dmitri staggered into her bedroom after bursting into the room. They glared at each other before he approached her. He was dressed in lounge pyjamas and a white shirt. The shirt was form fitting and made his chest look bulkier. Plus the pyjama bottoms made his torso look leaner. He really had an exquisite body of art. June gulped unsure what to do. Getting in bed or fleeing to the bathroom. None looked like the safe option.

"June." Dmitri said softly advancing into the room. June felt like a caged tiger so she backed away.

"June." Dmitri repeated as he was advancing very carefully toward her.

June looked around her bedroom for an escape route. There were few options. She decided to do the plain sight escape run. As Dmitri came up to her she ducked around him and ran. Her plan was almost perfect except for her assailant's quick reflexes. He grabbed her from behind and carried her to the bed.

She lay there trapped under him.

"I was going to leave you alone tonight but that stunt deserves some punishment. Plus I had forgiven you for the bite you gave me earlier. This stunt is really pushing the boundary line June." Dmitri looked at his arm which showed no sign of any bite.

"Since I am a fair man, I will give you three chances to redeem yourself." Dmitri was staring at her and talking very huskily in his heavily accented voice. June gulped as his voice dripped with sexual tension.

"I'm sorry?" June said not feeling sorry at all. She almost let out a little giggle.

Dmitri laughed, " Wrong answer try again."

"I will be good, could you release me now?" June knew Dmitri was just humouring her as he appeared in no hurry to let her go.

"One more chance." he stated smiling devilishly.

She put on her serious face but her lips refused to stop quivering.

"Well," she swallowed nervously. "I will listen to you and rest. Since I'm still a bit tired I will sleep with no objections."

Dmitri smiled in victory, " Wrong answer again, my darling June."

His head descended and he captured her lips. A frizzle zipped through her as their lips merged. She whimpered as he put his tongue into her mouth, June was lost. She wound her arms around his neck and pulled his head closer. He started to suck on her bottom lip; it was so erotic and sensual.

His teeth lightly grazed a trail to her jawbone and down to her neck. He left soft bites along her throat that made June tingle all over.

His tongue then dipped into her collarbone and she screamed with joy. He pushed the night shirt she was wearing over her head and captured her breasts in his hands. June was on fire. Her body was responding to his touch so effortlessly. She let out soft whimpers as Dmitri's tongue did things to her body that should be illegal.

"You seem to be enjoying your punishment a little bit too much Ms Stapleton." Dmitri said laughingly as she was recovering from yet another orgasm.

" My captor appears to be quite the tease!" she countered breathlessly.

"Is that so?" he smiled wickedly. He knelt over her and pulled off his shirt. June's body went into overdrive at seeing his rippled chest. He was so tanned and muscular when did he get the time to work out. Dmitri removed his bottoms and June knew she would be boneless by the time Dmitri was done with her. He was already hard with want.

He lay down next to her and guided her hand to his shaft. June had never touched a man so intimately before. She tentatively held him and he showed her what to do. June was marvelling at how easily Dmitri had become her slave and she was his master. She learnt how to please him and loved it when he buckled when her tongue touched a certain place.

" You slay me my darling June." Dmitri said hungrily as his trembling hand was struggling to put on a condom.

"To heck with it!" he said throwing the condom away after a third failed attempt to put it on. He grabbed her and making her straddle him as they joined. She rode him hard and fast and their mating was fierce. They both craved each other as the sexual heat was released through their union.

June got up to use the toilet. She was still tired. Sex with Dmitri had been out of this world. Her body still had that tingly feeling all over. She never thought that being with him could be so overwhelming and fulfilling. She looked at him asleep. His hair was falling over his forehead. He was too handsome for his own good. His mouth was curved slightly in a smile. That mouth was dangerous.

He had a square jawline and a shadow of a beard. He would look handsome with one she thought. She was still undecided about telling him about their child. She just did not trust him fully as yet. Maybe if she spent more time with him she would decide what to do soon.

She looked at the clock it was 5:45 am. June knew that this was her best chance so she took it.

Chapter 12

Pic of June and her sisters....May and April.

June had ignored the countless phone calls she had seen on her phone from Dmitri. After escaping her flat earlier she was now behind her desk catching up on work. She had missed the office and was feeling much better. She was speaking to Jay in the foyer after coming out to use the toilet for the umpteenth time this morning.

She had sent Dmitri a text earlier demanding that he move out as he was not welcomed in her flat anymore. She had not dared look at his response or take his calls since then.

"Jay you need to ensure that the resort is properly secured. Make sure that the contractors and workmen follow protocol and the paperwork is always up to date." She was briefing him because he would be managing this project on site while she was stuck in the office.

"Sure June, I will follow the pin point list you designed." Jay responded.

"Come into my office while I show you how to do it." Jay followed her into her office.

"Lucy, please remind me when my 11 am appointment arrives." June reminded her secretary before closing her office door.

She took out the plans for Dmitri's retreat project and placed them on her table.

"Have a look at this here Jay, the ratio of time and action is important to ensure that the project remains on time target." June always enjoyed her job. "If time is spent too long on one project the whole project will suffer financially and emotionally."

"Wow June, it is a lot of work. Mr Kanaredes is a huge client but I will certainly do my best." Jay said a bit nervously.

" I know you will otherwise you would not have been chosen." June tried to soothe a nervous Jay. " Look at this proposal here, if we begin with this section first it will make the process simpler."

"That is definitely a plus. Is Elsa from the junior department coming with me?" Jay asked

"Yes plus Luke is on standby if extra man power is needed." June added, "I trust the two of you to complete the start of this project we can further assess the project after you arrive in Sicily and report on your findings."

June sipped from her a glass of water, "Sicily is a gorgeous place, you are lucky to be travelling there."

"I hear the weather is very tropical so I will bring along enough shorts and t shirts." Jay said jokingly

"Hey not too much play, Hamilton would have my head on a chopping block if something goes wrong with this."

"No worries I will bring my sun block as well." Jay said deliberately misinterpreting her words.

Her phone rang, but she was hesitant to pick it up in case it was Dmitri.

"Aren't you getting that?" Jay asked on the fifth ring.

June reluctantly picked up her phone, she smiled in relief at the caller id.

" Hi sis," she greeted.

"Hi sis my foot! June you are in big trouble!" Her younger sister May said angrily.

"Hmm." June responded aware that Jay was in the room.

"So it's like that now." May continued

"I am at work right now."

"Work? Mom said you were holed up in your flat with some handsome rich guy who had gotten you preggers!"

"May , I can't talk now." June glanced at Jay who was smiling and gesturing to her to continue with her call as he made himself comfortable on the sofa while flipping through the file he was holding.

"Let's talk later," she tried to get her sister to end the call

"Fine, see you at lunchtime, be ready to reveal all big sis!" with that May hang up.

"Sorry about that Jay," June apologised.

May was the troublemaker in the family as the middle child she was the one who did all the antics. May was a fashion designer. She was into clothes and runways and makeup. June was lost in her world but May enjoyed it to bits. She was always travelling for Fashion shows in Paris or Milan or New York but May preferred to be at her desk designing new styles. She was not famous as yet but was having some success working with renowned designer Donna Karan London. June had been to a few fashion shows and even marketed some but the fashion world was one genre she had not mastered as yet.

It was already 12.20 pm and June would be meeting May at La Tasca, a Spanish restaurant which was nearby. May had already texted that she was five minutes away. June was rushing for the lift. It was a bit crowded in the lobby as many people were waiting for the lift to go to lunch.

When she heard the lift open, her body stiffened and became tense. She just knew who had walked out of the lift. She tried to blend in with the crowd as Dmitri and Franco came out. His eyes focused on her immediately and he came to face her. The crowd parted like the Red Sea for him. He looked dashing in his three piece grey suit. A waist coat was made for him.

"Ms Stapleton." He greeted. She could see that he was angry. His eyes were almost black and his jaw was set.

"Good afternoon Mr Kanaredes, Franco." June greeted politely as she rushed into the closing lift. As the doors closed the last image that she saw was Dmitri's furious face scowling at her.

June exhaled as she exited the building. She knew that Dmitri would not let this go but now she had another matter to face with her sister.

May was already at their table when she arrived at the restaurant. It was very exotic and the dark wooden furniture made the place have a real rustic feel to it. They were seated in a private area and June noticed that April was also there. She walked over to her sisters and hugged them. May was slim and tall. Her mahogany hair was stylishly layered to her shoulders. Her grey eyes were her best feature as it made her face look elf like. April resembled their father the most, she had a square jaw and green eyes. Her hair was cut in the same short pixie hair cut like hers but it was blonde. April was working in a law firm but had one year left of law school.

June sat in the cubicle and ordered some lemon juice; her sisters already had drinks in front of them.

"So who is he?" asked May curiously.

"How far are along are you?" April asked simultaneously.

June held up her hands, "I can only answer one question at a time."

"Me first!" shouted May, "What is his name and where did you meet him?"

"His name is Dmitri, he is Greek and we met accidentally a few weeks ago."

May looked at her quizzically not satisfied with the response.

"Come on June you just told me everything I already know."

"Next question, April." June looked at her other sister ignoring May's death stare.

" How many weeks are you?" April asked more seriously.

" Almost seven weeks and the morning sickness is no joke!" June responded laughingly.

May was still fuming but ready with her next question.

"Okay, now tell us what we do not already know!" May was insistent.

"Who is this Greek guy, what does he do and why is he staying in your flat?" May rattled on quickly.

June was smiling her sisters seemed to want to know everything. She did not blame them usually the shoe was on the other foot. She was the one firing questions at their deeds.

"He runs a shipping company and is very arrogant and domineering and a basic bully." June went on a rant about Dmitri.

"He can be so frustrating in getting his own way. He moved into my flat with his PA, a chef and a maid because he wanted to be 'near' me in case I was sick." Her sisters looked at each other and smiled, "I mean who does that kind of thing? I was a prisoner in my own home."

"So you are in love with him?" May asked smiling wickedly.

"Oh gosh no! I barely know him plus he lied to me when we first met." June was confused, she had not thought of her feelings for Dmitri.

"He lied?" April inquired. Her legal ears tuned to the statement.

June told them the story of how she and Dmitri had met at the cottage.

"Okay so now you are pregnant for this Greek billionaire and you are afraid to tell him because…?" May was waiting for an answer.

June did not know what to say, why was she really not telling Dmitri about her pregnancy? At first she felt it was because she was angry with him but now what was her reason? What future did she and Dmitri have? The point is that she did not know and she was still confused about her future and this baby.

"I don't know, we barely know each other and well I'm afraid how he will react if I tell him that I am expecting his child." June admitted finally.

April held her hand on the table, " It is okay to be scared J but he is the father and he does have a right to know about his child."

She squeezed her sister's hand feeling her support, " Thanks A, I realise that I need to do something but we barely have a relationship and right now I'm just coping with this news and the morning sickness more like all day sickness and well we haven't really talked."

"Then speak to him and do it soon." April encouraged lovingly.

"He is really angry at me right now though." Her sisters looked at her with confusion in their eyes.

June explained to them the escape to the office at 6 am and the encounter near the lift.

May was in stitches by the time she was finished relaying the events.

"June, I never thought you had it in you!" May was laughing loudly now.

" Oh May every since I met Dmitri I have been doing strange things." June acknowledged thinking that Dmitri made her irrational.

They ate their meal in laughter with June being the brunt of jokes. It was nice to be with her siblings. She had missed their presence. June had learned that vegetables were the only food she could keep down with no protest from her stomach to which her sisters had a lot to say. Her sisters agreed to go home with her in the evening to face Dmitri but she knew that they just wanted to meet him. June agreed as there was force in numbers. Plus she had made up her mind to discuss her pregnancy with Dmitri soon.

They had met in the lobby of her block of flats. Of course May had arrived first. April was a bit late but June did not mind as delaying the inevitable was ok for her. She had received one call from Dmitri in the afternoon which she had not answered and a text which followed soon after informed her to meet him in the evening at 8 pm at an address near Primrose Hill. She had not replied and had hoped that maybe he was out of her flat.

June opened her flat hesitantly and noticed that her flat was empty. No Dmitri or his office scattered throughout her living area. The place was spotless but empty. June was relieved but wary at the same time.

"He is gone bummer!" May moaned flopping on the sofa.

"June are you okay?" April asked sensing that her sister was looking pale. April guided her to the sofa and got her a glass of water. June does not know came over her she somehow was surprised that Dmitri was gone.

"That is a relief." June finally said. She got up and went to her bedroom. Her sisters followed her. She turned around and smiled.

"I can sleep in peace tonight." June said as she flopped onto the bed.

"J be real being alone in a bed is not peace.... it is torture!" May added as she also flopped onto the bed.

"I do not ask you details about your sex life so stay out of mine." June admonished her sister.

"I'm sure he must be great in bed to have my big sis look so disappointed he has gone!" May laughed and scooted away as June lunged for her. April was the voice of reason and said,

"June you are pregnant be more careful!" that was like cold water onto June. She sat up and realised that she was starving.

"Indeed sis I'm hungry what can we eat!" she proclaimed loudly standing up.

"Why don't you call him?" May was asking not letting the matter of Dmitri go.

"No!" June was adamant.

"Why not you said you were going to discuss the pregnancy with him so why not tonight." May was right but June was not ready.

"Not tonight, tonight my sisters and I are having a girls' night. It's Friday!" she cheered.

"Fine but tomorrow you need to call him J okay?" May said giving her a hug.

"Fine M." June conceded. She would have one more night before she told Dmitri of his impending fatherhood.

They had ordered pizza and strangely the vegetable pizza was staying down as well as the garlic bread.

They had showered and changed into June's casual clothes. They were sitting on the living room floor munching and chatting away when the doorbell rang. It must be the delivery guy to deliver the indian food they had ordered. May volunteered to answer the door.

June used the opportunity to make another trip to the toilet. The urinating thing every five minutes was tiring. Her bladder appeared to have been on constant drip.

"Is the food here?" June asked coming back into the room. She stilled as she noticed Dmitri sitting on the sofa with her sisters on either side of him. He was dressed in his usual suit attire minus the tie and waist coat. It was a dark blue one different to the one he had on earlier.

May was the first to talk, her face filled with mischief, "Hey J guess who decided to visit."

Chapter 13

June walked slowly to the empty sofa opposite her siblings and a curious looking Dmitri. He did not look angry but she could tell he was annoyed with her.

"Do not worry J we have already introduced ourselves and Dmitri here had kindly decided to join our girls' night." May was enjoying this too much.

"Hey M chill!" April voiced realising that May was having too much fun at her other sister's expense.

"Dmitri what brings you here at this time?" June looked at her wall clock it was almost 10 pm. Dmitri had probably realised she would not come to their appointment.

"Did you forget we were supposed to meet at 8 pm dear?" He said sweetly but his voice stressed on the dear a bit too much.

"Silly me, being sick and all I tend to forget easily especially when it's not really important." June responded just as sweetly.

Her sisters were watching the exchange with animated expressions. Dmitri cleared his throat and stood up. He walked over to June and sat beside her on the love seat. She tried to pull away but he grabbed her hand keeping her locked next to him. June heard a snicker and saw May smiling. The wretch.

"So Dmitri our sister has told us very little and I mean very little about you." May continued using her right thumb and index finger to demonstrate her point.

Dmitri looked uncomfortable for once.

"Fine but Dmitri tell us about yourself." May continued,

"Um what do you want to know?" Dmitri asked.

"First is it true you kidnapped our sister when you first met." May asked sitting Indian style on the sofa.

"M!" June reprimanded.

"It's okay we had a rough start. I guess a beautiful woman walking into your home drenched and muddy saying she is lost in the middle of the night can raise some eyebrows." Dmitri answered and they all laughed except June who had been blushing; relishing in the fact that Dmitri had found her be

"To top it off she walks in on you just coming from the shower." Dmitri continued with a sparkle in his eye.

"So technically the kidnapping was justified." May said laughter in her voice.

"Indeed." Dmitri agreed.

"I could tend to agree." April conceded and June glared at her. She thought at least one of her siblings would take her side. April shrugged her shoulders. June was blushing immeasurably.

"June you never told us that part." May was enjoying this immensely. "You made him into this Sopranos Mafia guy who had his henchmen keep you locked in a basement room chained to the wall with no food or water for days." May was exaggerating beyond belief.

"You are being ridiculous, M" June said finally extracting her hand from Dmitri's grasp.

"Would you like something to drink Dmitri?" April offered breaking the banter.

"Sure after being stood up tonight I need something strong to calm my broken heart." Dmitri was totally annoying her now with his melodrama.

"Beer?" April offered, "Sorry that's all we have for broken hearts tonight."

"Thanks." Dmitri accepted.

"Now June how could you not tell us that you had a date with Dmitri tonight?" May shook head as April delivered the beer.

"We would have made her go if we knew." May was saying to Dmitri becoming his ally.

"Please until Dmitri appeared you were dissing him as well!" June countered annoyed with her siblings 180 degree turn.

"Dmitri, we were misinformed so we made a biased judgement against you which we have since revised based on current information." May stated with a stoic voice. Her face full of mischief and glee.

"Traitor!" June was fed up with her sisters turning against her.

What was it with Dmitri and his charm?

"I'll forgive you dear," Dmitri was lounging and tapping the spot next to him "If you wanted to spend time with your sisters you could have told me so, by phone perhaps?"

"Oh please as if you would have listened, you steam rolled into my home and now you are trying to charm my sisters against me."

"Hey J, I am still on your side." April piped up.

"Please!" she countered as May and Dmitri laughed.

"My opinion is still open J so it's ok." April again had her legal cap on.

"Thanks let's disown M." they all laughed.

"I'm curious as to your names." Dmitri asked looking at them curiously.

"It's cool don't you think, we are all born in the months of which we are named. Our parents thought it would be cool and it so is!" June shook her head May was in her element as she explained their name origins.

"Nice, what do you do May?" Dmitri continued his inquisition. Everyone was now more relaxed as the conversation flowed nicely.

"I am a fashion designer, I love fashion and I must say that your suit is definitely a custom made Armani and the shoes are probably custom made as well." May was saying a she used her fashion sense.

"I see you know your designers. What about you April?"

"I work in a law firm and I am in my last year of law school so if you want to mess with my sister I think you better tread carefully."

"I will remember that surely." Dmitri smiled wistfully.

"Hmmm, so Dmitri when June told us about you today." May stressed on the word and looked at Dmitri with a smirk, "I googled you and apart from being a 'rich guy who is a bully' you own a large corporation but as someone with such vast resources and contacts. I have never seen you at any fashion shows or galas?"

Dmitri glanced at June and smiled.

"Ah I see June has been very forthcoming about me." He grinned "I value my privacy and I guess that was one reason I was very apprehensive when I first met your sister. I run a large business and I need to protect my staff and their jobs. I can be a workaholic and my father taught me the value of productiveness. I was not always wealthy so I guess I value hard work. So my effort is not only for me but for those who work with and for me. I confess it can take a lot for me to give up working."

June had learnt something new about Dmitri; the way he spoke about his father showed that he had great respect for him. In addition his work ethic was exemplary. She had seen it herself over the last two days. He was very dedicated and hands on. He ensured that things happened in his company and he appeared to be involved in whatever was being done in any company in any part of the world. No wonder he spoke so many languages; it showed that he wanted to connect more with his companies around the world. Something in her heart swelled for Dmitri. He had shown how caring he was for his employees. June decided that she would tell him about their baby. He would be a good father, maybe he would be hands on.

"June your family are great, I guess I will be meeting more of them tomorrow." Dmitri said waking her from her reverie.

"Tomorrow? Are you coming to the barbecue?" April asked surprised.

"Yes your parents invited me." June could not believe this.

"Great, we will see you tomorrow Dmitri." May stifled a yawn. "I am wiped out, I need my beauty sleep, come on A, time to say nighty nighty."

May practically dragged April out of the flat. June was left alone with Dmitri who was sipping his beer slowly and smiling.

June closed the door and took a deep breath. She had to talk to Dmitri tonight. "Your sisters are fun. It must have been great growing up with them."

"Yeah it was." June was cleaning up and throwing things in the bin. She was unsure how to begin the conversation. She stood by the sink and rinsed the dishes before placing them in the dishwasher. She turned around and Dmitri grabbed her.

He barricaded her against the kitchen counter.

"So June can you tell me why you keep running away from me?"

June swallowed and lowered her head. Dmitri raised her head and gently kissed her lips.

"You get me so mad by your actions but when I have you in my arms all I want to do is kiss your tender lips and make love to you. You fill my head with your body writhing against mine; I can barely concentrate on my work." He was kissing her neck. "I don't know what you are doing to me June but I have never been so affected by a woman like this." He was now moulding her breast under her shirt. June was putty in his hands. "So June tell me how you have bewitched me." June whimpered as his tongue trailed around her collarbone. June gripped his shoulders as passion zipped through her body. The man was the one who had her in a spell.

"Dmitri we need to talk...." he squeezed her nipples and nipped at her neck.

"....mmmmm." Dmitri had now removed her shirt and his hands and mouth were doing magic to her body.

"We...mmm....need....mmm...to...talk..." June was swimming in sensual pleasure. The man knew how to use his tongue.

"What do you want to say?" Dmitri asked embracing her and carrying her to the bed.

He deposited her on the bed and stood back. He removed his shirt and undid his trousers. He was more than ready and June was speechless.

June could not talk she lay there in her underwear staring at the fine specimen of male before her....her heart was beating so fast. Dmitri came to her, he stretched out his hand and she came to her knees on the bed in front of him. He kissed her fingers and sucked on them.

"June what do you want to say...." He asked again. June pulled him to her and kissed him firmly.

"Let's talk later." She decided as they fell onto the bed and got lost in each other.

June was getting ready for the barbecue. Dmitri had left early to deal with some business. He would be picking her up in 15 minutes. June was feeling much better, the morning sickness had decided to be good to her and it was receding. She was undecided what shoes to wear. She stood in front of the mirror she was wearing a floral box pleat skater dress. It had a high scooped neckline and was sleeveless; so she carried a plain white shrug in case it got a bit chilly. June grabbed a pair of embellished silver gemstone sandals. They were flat and comfortable. She adjusted the straps knowing that Dmitri would be here any minute now.

The door bell sounded just as her phone rang.

"Hi," she answered rushing to the door.

She opened the door and stopped in shock as Dmitri's smooth voice responded, "I'm waiting downstairs."

June was dumbstruck as she stared at Gared in her doorway.

"You look fabulous June." He greeted, pulling her into a hug.

Chapter 14

This chapter is dedicated to Orchissa and MinHuHuo for your comments!!! Thanks so much.

Pic of Gared Thompson played by Brandon Routh.

June was speechless as she was enveloped into Gared's arms.

"I missed you June, I'm so glad to be back." He released her. "The business trip was long and tedious."

June finally regained her speech a she got out of Gared's embrace.

"Um Gared, it's great to see you but I have a previous appointment." She needed to get Gared away before Dmitri saw him.

"What? You forgot our date to go to the new art museum in Chelsea?" Gared looked crushed.

June had totally forgotten about him much less their date. She was becoming a horrible person; she had been dealing with too many things this past week. Her oh so boring life had become complicated.

"Well something came up, I'm headed to my family, we have this...um...meeting." June hated to lie to him but she did not know what to say at that point. They were in the lift heading downstairs.

"Okay, I guess family supersedes everything." He agreed readily. June breathed a sigh of relief.

"So can we reschedule for tomorrow." June was stuck. The lift opened and she was hoping Dmitri was in the car hidden away and not waiting outside on the pavement.

She tried to stall Gared as they exited the lift. June tried to walk ahead to ensure that the coast was clear. She noticed a black SUV parked at the entrance and no Dmitri in sight. She smiled and turned to Gared in relief.

"Sure I'll meet you tomorrow at 11 am. I have something to help my sister with so it's best I meet you at the museum since I will be in that part of the city." June was becoming the seasoned liar. She hated herself for it but she needed to buy herself a day at least.

"Sure, 11 am it is." He pulled her into another embrace; she made sure they were not visible from outside.

"Thanks for understanding, see you tomorrow."

Gared grabbed her hand, "Until tomorrow," he was going in for a kiss when her mobile rang. It must be Dmitri wondering where she was.

"Later." She said digging for her phone from her purse. She waved him good bye as she answered quickly.

"Yes, I'm almost there stop rushing me!" she shouted at Dmitri who had not said anything.

She ended the call and left the building. One of Dmitri's guards opened the back door for her as she entered the SUV.

"See right here!" she said arranging her seatbelt next to a very angry looking Dmitri who was waving his phone in his hand.

"June." He said in a controlled voice. She had to defuse the situation swiftly so she used her best weapon. She leaned over and kissed him and put on her most adorable face.

"Sorry?" she said softly. "You suit up well Kanaredes." She touched his jacket lapel and kissed him again.

Dmitri smiled at her and pulled her into a deeper kiss as they drove to her Aunt's home.

Dmitri appeared to have not seen Gared to which she was grateful but her nerves were in bundles. She needed to end it fully with Gared tomorrow and ensure Dmitri did not find out.

The place was buzzing with family and guests. She was a bit nervous for her family to meet Dmitri but he put a hand around her waist and gave her a light kiss.

"You look gorgeous in this dress June." He whispered in her ear.

Strangely, he appeared a bit nervous as well. Hmmm she thought.

He was casually dressed in dark blue jeans paired with a brown tweed blazer and waist coat and matching brown shoes. Was there an outfit he could not wear? The man was a model's envy.

"J over here!" May was already there with a drink in hand. She was nicely dressed in white Capri shorts and a batwing floral blouse. June went to her with Dmitri following closely behind.

She gave her sister a hug, "Hey M, you look great!"

"Me? You are glowing!" she gave May a stern look which was quickly shot down.

"Hi Dmitri, welcome!" Dmitri came to June's side as May greeted him.

"Thanks, great to be here." Dmitri stated looking around the place full of June's family.

"Come on let's circulate." May dragged June's hand into the crowd with Dmitri holding her other hand.

"Hey guess who arrived with company!" May announced to everyone.

Dmitri was greeted by her parents, and introduced to her Aunt Celia and Uncle Wyatt as well as other relatives. The men had dragged him away as June went to get a drink and a breather.

"It's okay sis, he will be fine!" May reassured her.

"I'm more worried about me surviving this day." She said as she recounted the Gared encounter earlier.

"Oh my sis is living the fast life." May laughed smiling wickedly. "They call me the wild one!"

"May, I do not appreciate the jibes, I just need some clarity." She was getting distraught.

"It is simple, you meet him tell him that you met someone else and move on. Simple." May said waving her hands like a conductor.

"Indeed but if Dmitri wants to see me then what do I say?" she asked worriedly.

"We'll figure it out but my sis is moving from no social life to too much?" May was enjoying this, she was the one who usually juggled two or three guys at once. She called them her fish pool.

"Okay what did I miss?" April joined their conversation.

"A lot!" May punctuated while filling in their other sister on the Gared development.

June had little time to even think of this some more as family ushered her from one place to another. Dmitri had been employed to be one of the grill masters. He appeared relaxed and to be enjoying himself. He had taken off his jacket and waistcoat and rolled up the sleeves of his white shirt. His jeans rode low on his hips. Oh the man was too fine for her beating heart. She looked at him and he winked at her. He tried to flip a burger over in style and he succeeded. His little fan club which were her teenage cousins all cheered. His ego swelled 100 notches as he repeated his feat. She shook her head as she approached him.

"So Mr show off does it taste good?" she teased as she grabbed a kebab skewer. She had just bit a morsel of red pepper off the skewer when Dmitri bit into it as well. She paused as he pulled off the meat chunk and snuck in a kiss before pulling the strip totally off the strip. The man was too much temptation.

She chewed slowly as Dmitri bit off another strip from her skewer.

"Hey get your own!" she chided and his female fan club cooed in amazement. June stared at them sternly and they scattered away.

"I am the cook I get to nibble whenever I want." Somehow his words went beyond barbecuing and the heat rose a notch and not from the fire.

"Do you want me to get you another beer?" she asked trying to leave the heated environment.

Dmitri pulled her to him, "Later." he whispered before saying "Thanks." He said and she knew exactly what he meant. She skirted out so quickly and got one of her male cousins to bring him the beer.

She was coming out of the bathroom when her mother met her and pulled her into the study and shut the door.

"How are you feeling today my dear?" her mother asked. She was beautifully dressed in a blue crochet shift dress.

"I'm getting the hang of it, the queasiness is subsiding and not everything wants to come out any more." She replied giving her mom a hug.

"Have you told him?" was the dreaded question she did not want to hear.

June stepped away from her mum and sat on the nearby leather sofa. She put her head in her hands.

"I can't seem to say it." She looked up at the mother in despair; her mother sat down next to her and held her hands. "I'm usually so strong and independent but with Dmitri I'm like all soppy and weak."

"Oh my dear, this is what happens when you release your heart." Her mother was being supportive.

"But mum, I don't know what to do any more." She moaned as she hugged her mum.

"Honey, I raised three very strong daughters. You found love and it's new but you can do this. You need to make it right. The sooner you tell him the better it will be. Dmitri is a fair man; he feels the same about you too. I can see it every time he looks at you."

"But mum we've barely known each other for a few months. It's too fast." She felt that things had been rushing so quickly.

"Honey, I knew your dad was the one at our first meeting. He took me on a date right after getting his driving licence and smashed into a parked car when he was trying to park at the restaurant." Her mother reminisced. "Your dad was so overwhelmed but he handled the situation brilliantly. He did not run away but dealt with the vehicle owner and the police as well. We ended up eating burgers from a fast food joint down the street all dressed up in our formal clothes."

Her mother patted her hand, "It was his sincerity in dealing with the situation which made me love him. He knew your grand-dad would make him pay for the damaged car but he faced it all."

"Dmitri was not always rich and he doesn't act all snobbery at all even if he is one of the world's richest men." June revealed.

"Exactly my child, once you see his sincerity hat is all that matters." Her mother's story made her think that she needed to give Dmitri a proper chance and face the future. June was also worried about the pregnancy and the responsibility that came with it.

"What kind of mother will I be I'm so afraid. I know nothing about raising a child.

You are a great woman June you have always been determined and you got your MBA and a blossoming career and you own your flat. You just need to find your balance again. You will be a great mother June, you had a good teacher." They smiled at each other and she hugged her mother tightly.

"Thanks Mom you are the best. Thank you."

Her mother left after one final hug. June knew she was being weak she had never been affected by a man the way Dmitri had totally bowled her over. She was going to be a mother and she had to make it work with Dmitri she was strong. June arrived in the kitchen to hear cheers. It seems the men had begun the notorious football match. Her dad versus her uncle. Her aunt lived across the street from an open communal space.

It was just a huge expanse of green grass that the locals used for any sport or pastime. June saw Dmitri in full football kit. Yes the men went all out every year. He was on her dad's team. He wore blue shorts which really showed off his muscular thighs and a blue shirt which said Team Martin on it.

June joined in the cheers. At the interval her dad was giving a firm pep talk since his team was down by one goal to her uncle's team which had two goals in the net. Her dad did not want to lose and by all the gesticulation going on in the team huddle she was sure he was pushing home that fact. Dmitri appeared to be giving pointers as well. Did he know anything about football? It appeared he did by the way the team were nodding.

The break was over and Team Wyatt pushed off with an easy goal to start, to lead by three goals to one. Team Wyatt had coordination and was passing the ball with ease. Team Martin was finding it hard to keep the ball and their defense were fighting hard to prevent another goal being scored against them. Dmitri called another timeout and he was animatedly showing something in the team huddle.

After the timeout Team Martin were on fire. Dmitri appeared to change his position on the restart and was now playing as a centre forward. Her Dad passed the ball to her cousin Eric who then flipped it over to Dmitri and he kicked it passed Uncle Wyatt who was his team's goalkeeper. Team Martin was still down with two goals to Team Wyatt. June cheered with her family. May had become an impromptu cheerleader along with Dmitri's teenage fan club and their voices were reigning out with encouragement. Before long her cousin Bernard on her Dad's team scored a goal it was a tie... three all.

The match was almost over and at this rate it was destined to be a draw with each team having three goals each.

Uncle Neve who was the referee shouted that there were two minutes left to play. Team Wyatt had possession of the ball. They were passing well and Cousin Luke on Team Wyatt kicked the ball but it deflected off the post. Everyone groaned at the miss. The game was back in play and Dmitri got the ball, he skilfully run with it away from Team Wyatt. He was near the goal but he was being blocked, he passed it to her dad who shuffled it in slowly and it went straight through Uncle Wyatt's hands. Goal! Followed by the final whistle. Team Martin had won!

Her Dad's team were exuberant. Everyone ran onto the field. June rushed to Dmitri who was still panting. She gave him a huge hug and a quick kiss.

"You were so awesome!" June shouted as Dmitri collapsed onto the field.

"That was amazing!" he said breathlessly. She handed him some water as her dad came over. Dmitri stood up and her dad gave him a huge handshake.

"Good team work Kanaredes!" her Dad complimented as he clapped Dmitri on the back.

"Thanks, sir." The two most important men in her life smiled at each other.

"You were magnificent Dad!" June said giving her Dad a hug.

"Thanks my sweet, your man here did good today." Her dad acknowledged before he walked off to cheers and chants. He had earned bragging rights for another year.

Chapter 15

Pic of Dmitri's bathroom and dressing room.

Dmitri was the entire buzz as they drove back to his house after the family gathering. He had decided to take her to his place. He owned a house in a quiet cul de sac in Belgravia, London. Her modest two bedroom flat looked meagre compared to the opulence that she was now standing in. The five bedroom house was spaced over four floors and had an indoor lift.

The place was furnished in light colours and was full of natural light. She was on the first floor in one of the guest bedrooms.

She had taken a quick shower in the en suite.

Strangely there were new clothes in her size laid out on the bed when she had entered the bedroom. She put on the red lace underwear which was a perfect fit. Then she held up a simple but elegant textured green skater dress. It fit like a glove. The fabric was so soft and caressed her skin. She smiled, Dmitri had good taste.

She climbed the padded stairs bare feet to the second floor. It held only the master bedroom. She entered the room and was taken aback by the space it encompassed. There was a huge king size bed and elegant furniture scattered throughout the room. She walked through the open door to a walk in closet on one side was for clothes and the other accessories and shoes. She continued walking and she peeked into the bathroom, Dmitri had his eyes closed and he appeared to have drifted off to sleep. He lay naked in the huge tub his head resting against the back and his arms spread out along the sides.

She went up to him and traced his jawline. It was firm and strong. She trailed her hand around his lips. He suddenly opened his mouth and captured her index finger. She yelped and tried to balance herself from falling inside the tub.

"Hey" she said as he held her finger and refused to release it.

He lightly nipped her finger before slowly opening his mouth. She let her finger trail down his chest.

"The clothes are lovely, thanks." He smiled

"Everything in the room belongs to you, you are special to me June." He said looking at her lovingly.

"Come on you look tired." She said as she handed him a towel and went to the bedroom. She had promised him a massage.

He came out a few minutes later naked.

She had placed another towel on the bed and had gotten some massage oils from his bathroom stock.

She pointed to the bed and he raised his eyebrows.

He lay down in the supine position smiling. His member already pointing upwards. She wriggled her finger for him to turn. He groaned but turned onto his stomach. June sat next to him as she poured some oil onto his back. He squirmed. She proceeded to massage his shoulders and his lower back as she reached his butt he bucked up. It was his sensitive spot.

She went over to his strong legs. She rubbed her hands over his firm thighs and went to his butt again he held her hands and flipped himself over. She straddled him as she massaged his chest. His member was standing proudly before her. June stood over him a leg planted on either side and pulled her dress over her head.

She then straddled him again. Dmitri was moaning as she took him into her mouth. He bucked under her as she took him in deeply. He tried to pull her under him but she wriggled her index finger at him

"It's my turn." She whispered against his mouth as she started to take control of their love making. She let him pull her knickers off with his teeth as she took him into her heated core. June had never felt so powerful yet so complete.

She woke up with the sun on her face. She squirmed; the lovemaking had been out of this world. She had gone further than ever before with Dmitri. She smiled as she reached for him and realised she was alone in the bed. There was a note on the side table with under her lace knickers.

"I'll need to get you a crotch less pair as you looked really hot in this! You blew my mind June. I need to return to Sicily today but I'll call you." D

She read the note three times before she eventually got out of bed. She was a bit annoyed he did not wake her before he left but she smiled maybe it was payback. She went to the guest room to shower when her mobile beeped. It was a message from Gared. Oh gosh she had totally forgotten about him.

"See you at 11." It read.

She looked at the time it was 9.30 am. She had overslept. She would not have time to go home and meet Gared. She looked into the closet there were all types of clothing. Formal, casual, business attire, everything. Did Dmitri expect her to move in with him? She decided on a cropped leg cobalt blue jumpsuit. It had a wrapped around blouse with a medium sash around the waist. She decided to keep her hair down and matched it with some black stiletto sandals. She hated wearing Dmitri's clothes to see Gared but she had little choice.

She arrived at the museum a little before 11 am. Dmitri's driver had insisted on taking her wherever she needed to go. The museum was surprisingly already buzzing with visitors. She was about to call Gared when she felt a hand around her waist.

"Morning lovely," Gared greeted her giving her a kiss on the cheek. June pulled away and faced him

"Hi." She said nervously

"You look beautiful." He continued guiding her into the museum.

"Thanks." June knew that she had to tell him today that they had no future.

They began the tour. The art exhibit was beautiful. The pieces were commissioned by the Duke of Westminster and designed by various artists from Camberwell Gallery. The pieces were a reflection of Victorian England. June loved the reflective pieces. Gared was a good conversationalist and she was enjoying herself rather guiltily.

They were sitting in the café outside the gallery museum. It was a mild day and the weather was lovely.

"So June when can we do this again?" Gared said holding her hand.

June pulled her hand away.

She cleared her throat and looked at the gorgeous man in front of her. She would have given him a chance if Dmitri had not met her first.

"Um. Gared, well, you see I'm dating someone else." She blurted out. Gared put his cup of coffee down rather slowly before adjusting in his chair.

"I did not mean to lead you on but I met him again after I met you and well we decided to start something and well. I'm sorry." June rushed out unable to look at Gared.

There was silence from his side for a few minutes and she looked up at him. He was staring at her his face showing mixed emotions.

"I'm really really sorry Gared." She continued trying to make him understand.

"That was a shocker." He finally said quietly.

"I like you as a friend, you are a really nice guy but -"he cut her off

"But you are not attracted to me." He appeared very hurt

"So how long have you been with this other guy." He asked

"Not long but it's just that we were over and then he came back and now..." she drifted off.

"I'm shocked June I really thought we had something. I guess I was too late." Gared was really sounding hurt.

"I'm truly sorry." Gared stood up and she followed suit.

"See you around June." He said walking away from her. June sat back down, she felt really awful. Gared was a real nice guy.

Suddenly she was pulled up and Gared held her arms "I need to do this first before I go." June looked at him stunned as to what was going to happen. He captured her head in his hands and pulled her to him. He kissed her on the mouth. Since her mouth was open he put in his tongue. June did not kiss him back but he released her slowly and she stared at him speechless.

"I needed at least a kiss. Goodbye June." He said leaving her standing there quite shocked. June tried to gather herself and picked up her purse and rushed to the bathroom to calm down.

She did not hear from Dmitri all week. Jay had left on Wednesday to meet him in Sicily. June as a bit peeved that Dmitri had not contacted her and she would definitely not contact him first. He had left so it was on him to contact her. Her nerves were frayed by the time the week ended. Every time her phone rang or beeped she got on edge but still no contact from the great Kanaredes.

He was still alive because Jay had communicated with he office that he had met him but was he so busy that he ignored her. June touched her stomach was this a sign. He was such a workaholic that out of sight out of mind was his policy.

"Oh baby! She said holding her hand against her still flat tummy.

"Your daddy is making mummy very angry."

May had told her that she was over dramatizing everything and that Dmitri was still into her but busy. She tried to feel reassured that he was indeed a busy man but at least a short text would suffice.

June got another project and immersed herself into it to forget Dmitri. Two weeks had passed and no contact from him. She decided that when he did return she would definitely have a word with him about keeping contact. She had still not told him about the baby and as she sat in the doctor's office she was told that the pregnancy was going smoothly. Since she had hit her second trimester the morning sickness had disappeared and her appetite was starting to kick back in.

A little over a month after Dmitri had left she was summoned to Mr Hamilton's office. She walked in and was stunned to see Dmitri seated there with Franco and Jay. They were back. He looked so tanned and handsome in his three piece navy blue suit.

June composed herself and sat down. She refused to look at Dmitri. She held her files against her stomach defensively. She was not showing as yet but she needed the added protection. Jay smiled at her brightly and she returned the smile.

"Mr. Kanaredes I am so pleased that you are delighted with the progress of the project and that you want our team to continue in Sicily." Mr Hamilton stated happily.

"Indeed, Mr. Watson is a good worker and he handled the onsite business quite well. I would like him to continue until the end of the Sicily project." Dmitri said firmly.

He appeared calm too clam like a lion ready to pounce. He looked at her angrily and she was confused. He was angry at her? Why? What did she do to upset him? He was the one who had not called or texted or even communicated with her for over a month! She had to use her conversations with Jay to pull out any information about him and he was angry. As if! June forced herself up. She was hungry. She looked at her watch it was 12:45, she was just going to grab some lunch when she was called to Mr. Hamilton's office.

She rubbed her stomach and said silently in her head. "A few more minutes baby." Her unborn child was a stickler for eating times.

"June are you okay with this arrangement?" Mr. Hamilton was looking at her and so was everyone else. She was lost and looked around her she had drifted off into her own thoughts. Dmitri raised an eyebrow at her she blinked and turned to her boss

"Um well sir could you repeat that?" she hated to look unprofessional in front of Dmitri but she had no choice.

"Mr Kanaredes would like Jay to continue working on the project with the team in place, as head of department are you willing to release Jay for a few more months."

"That is fine we have handled his absence so far quite well we have delegated to some junior employees who appeared to be taking on the work superbly."

"That is settled then." Dmitri stood up. He shook hands with Mr. Hamilton. June stood up quickly and felt a bit light headed. She sat back down again and held her head.

"You okay June?" Jay asked coming to her side

"Yeah I'm fine." she tried to reassure him, "Let's have some lunch."

June got up again. Dmitri was staring at her and she glared him before everything went black.

Chapter 16

Pic of Rachel McAdams playing June.

She was lying on her couch when she came to. Dmitri was kneeling next to her. She looked at him disoriented, unsure why she was there.

'Are you ok?' he asked and it all came back to her. She tried to sit up but he kept her down. "Just remain as you are."

'You will be alright Ms. Stapleton, just relax, this is common for someone in your condition.' Dmitri leaned back and the company nurse came into view, she bent down and continued speaking,

"I guess you need to be more careful, the first trimester is a delicate one."

June was upset, the nurse, the baby; she put her hand to her stomach instinctively,

'You just need to have a bit of a rest,' the nurse continued as she made her way to the huge oak desk in the centre of the room.

June wanted to disappear; the nurse had just revealed that she was pregnant. She avoided Dmitri's gaze as she struggled to sit up, he helped her as she swung her legs off the couch. She was further mortified by Mr. Hamilton's presence in the room. He was studying her strangely. She could only imagine what he was thinking.

June just wanted to get away, out of this place, away from all the questioning eyes around her. She could not handle the curious glances.

'I feel much better now.' she offered weakly her voice sounding like an echo to her ears.

'Sorry for the trouble.' she continued trying to stand up, conscious of Dmitri helping her. She fixed her clothes and thanked the nurse.

'Mr. Kanaredes was very worried when you refused to regain consciousness; he said that you had been pale before you fainted.' The nurse said. June cringed inside at those words,

"I was a bit light headed but I feel fine now." She wanted the ground to swallow her up.

"When I checked you I realised that it was just your condition. You need to be more careful, have you seen your doctor?" the nurse asked kindly.

"Yes I saw him this morning." She stated, looking at the floor. When was this nightmare going to end?

The nurse smiled, "Just ensure that you take it easy, try not to work too hard." She excused herself and left. June was left with her boss and the one man she didn't want near her right now.

"Ms. Stapleton, I guess I must congratulate you on your pregnancy."

'Mr. Hamilton, I... thank you.' she stopped aware that Dmitri was now standing immediately behind her. She felt his coat brush her back as he moved. She froze.

"Well it is a happy time especially the first one." Mr. Hamilton had no idea; she could feel the tension emanating from Dmitri's body it was ice cold.

'I remember when my wife had our first she had a miserable first few months but afterwards things were okay, so be strong enjoy this wonderful time.' he continued going to his desk.

June followed his movements avoiding the volcano that was standing behind her.

'In light of this, June take the rest of the day off." He directed the next statement to Dmitri, "Sorry about the inconvenience Mr Kanaredes.' her boss said looking behind her for confirmation, she held her breath waiting.

'Actually Mr. Hamilton I would like to take Ms. Stapleton home,' Dmitri said forcefully and Mr. Hamilton looked puzzled back and forth at them.

June cringed further, the monster was about to pounce, he held her arm bit too tightly,

"That is fine Mr. Kanaredes," Mr Hamilton looked puzzled. "Are you feeling much better?" she shook her head in agreement and he smiled,"Good, then I will leave you two; be careful and remember to rest Ms Stapleton."

"Thank you Mr. Hamilton," June whispered looking at the floor.

Dmitri guided her taut body out of the room; Jay and Franco came in with her bag and coat. Mr. Hamilton looked at them quizzically, wondering what was up but he said nothing just nodded as they vacated the office. Dmitri guided her to the elevator; she numbly followed him trying not to bring any undue attention their way. He said nothing as Franco punched the button for the ground floor. She knew that he was waiting for a private place to unleash his fury; she was gearing herself for it.

Outside a black Range Rover with heavily tinted windows was parked at the building entrance. Dmitri opened the back door for her. She got in and Dmitri followed. Franco got in at the front as the driver set off for her apartment. She was silent all the way to her apartment. Dmitri was busy on his mobile and intermittently shouting out instructions to Franco. They were speaking in Greek rather quickly. She could not understand a word being said. Franco was multi-tasking, he was using a tablet and on his mobile while listening to Dmitri all at the same time. June closed her eyes she just needed to get away from all this. She entered her apartment and rushed to the kitchen to get a drink of water. Dmitri took off his coat and immediately went to the clear glassed drinks cabinet and took out a bottle of bourbon. He drank one shot before he turned to look at her scathingly.

She took the initiative 'Don't hold it inside any longer just let it out.' He poured another glass his shoulders taut with unreleased fury.

'I suppose, I wasn't going to be told?' he asked rhetorically.

'Why would I have to tell you about my pregnancy?' she challenged him, he drank more slowly this time.

'It's mine June, my child growing inside you and I have a right to know!' he slowly raised his voice and slammed the glass down.

"Don't act like you care!" she shouted back.

He turned towards her his face furious and clouded.

"Care? You dare use those words to me?" he came towards her, "All I have ever done is care June when you were sick in the cottage and again in this very flat."

"Oh please!" she said exasperatedly stuffing some crackers in her mouth. She was still hungry.

"Is the child mine June?' he continued coming toward her like a tiger stalking its prey. She cowered behind the kitchen counter holding the surface for support. She stood there staring at him; his eyes were alive with fury as he walked up the steps.

'I am waiting for an answer June?'

She tried to skirt away but he was already beside her his fury emanating him from in droves.

'Answer me!' he said softly but firmly, she was afraid to speak this man before had so much power and control what would happen to her now, her life would never be the same, she would be his, her child would be raised as his heir taken away from her. She shuddered to think how she would have no influence on her child. She wanted this baby to be hers; she had that right not him with his power and influence. She wanted a normal life not one ruled by Demetrious Tzarch von Kanaredes.

She mustered up all her courage as she said,

'Dmitri let's not do this.' she responded softly

His eyes turned almost black 'So it's that guy's the one you ran to after coming straight from my bed!'

He held her shoulders tightly, "You were seeing us both June at the same time!" he continued "How could you use me like this!"

"Does he know? Whose baby is this June mine or his?!" Dmitri had released her but he was standing so close, June felt suffocated and enclosed. Her head was heavy she could barely understand what Dmitri was saying. He was talking about a guy?

"Which guy?" she asked confused.

"Which guy? Is there more than one you are sleeping with now?" he insinuated laughing scornfully.

June shook her head dazed. "I don't know what you are saying." She had to move away from him, she blinked trying to get her head clear.

"The guy you went to the museum with the same day you left my bed." Came the angry voice in front of her.

June paused; she had only been to the museum with Gared. How did Dmitri know about it?

"Gared? What does he have to do with this?" she said still unsure why he was bringing this issue up.

Dmitri looked at her square on, "You met him at the museum and you kissed him in front of everyone." He revealed with a murderous look in his eyes.

"No I did not!" she denied unsure how he knew all this.

"I was breaking up with him!" her mind raced back to that day.

"So you admit you were seeing us both!" Dmitri backed away and ruffled his hair. He was pacing. His fists clenched at his sides. He stopped and punched the counter. June flinched.

"No... yes... well not really... Dmitri please, it was not what you are thinking!" she went to hold his arm. He pulled away from her and she stumbled backwards.

"You went out with him that day right out of my bed, how could you June! I met your family for crying out loud!" Dmitri was so angry that he was pacing. He glared at her menacingly while shaking his head.

She kept silent, she was still trying to process what Dmitri had said. How did he know about Gared? He was in Sicily. How did he know? Was this the reason he had not contacted her? Over a misunderstanding?

"Did you kiss him June?" Dmitri was asking.

She looked at him hazily, "Yes, I mean no, he kissed me. It was a mistake." She was still trying to process everything.

"You admit it so easily, I thought the pictures were a lie. I prayed that they were because I could not believe you would do this to us, to me!" Dmitri was shouting.

June tried to make sense of this in her haze, pictures where did he get pictures? That means..... he had her followed! Did he not trust her? He had his men to follow her without telling her. How dare he? June looked at him pacing in front of her angrily. She was now fired up, the man dared treat her like this and he was angry!

"Dmitri, you had me followed?" June asked her mind making sense of the information she was hearing. Dmitri stopped pacing and looked at her.

"Of course you were my woman I needed to keep you safe --."

June interrupted him, "No you had me followed! Without telling me, you had people to watch me?"

Dmitri held up his hands in protest and pointed his finger at her,

"You betrayed me June, you were with another man!"

"You betrayed me Dmitri?" He turned away from her. "You lied to me from the beginning about who you were. You have been treating me like a criminal from day one."

"I had to keep you safe!" he responded controlled, "I am a powerful man I needed to protect you!"

"Safe? Keeping me safe does not mean having one of your lackeys trail my every move. How dare you do that without my permission!" June walked to the living area; she needed to be away from him.

"It was for your safety but the point is you were caught out kissing another man June a few hours after you had been having sex with me in my bed!" Dmitri countered. "You let him touch what belonged to me!"

June threw her hands up; she sat on the sofa her feet feeling unsteady. Dmitri was incredible.

"Is that why you did not contact me in over a month? Is that why you are angry? You saw some pictures taken by your 'protection team' and assumed I was guilty!" she was fuming. The bastard actually was angry after what he did.

"You never trusted me Dmitri! You did things your own way as usual!" she was so furious she was seeing blue. Her head was so heavy and clouded. She had never been so disgusted or angry in her entire life. The man had finally done it. He had crossed the barrier and she wanted him out. Dmitri had gone too far this time.

"June, the issue here is you cheating on me and who fathered the child that you are carrying?" Dmitri was seating opposite her now, his elbows on his knees and his hands on the either side of his head.

June stared back at him blankly. Did she want this life? Would she be happy with him? Is that how he worked? He wanted to control her, keep her caged. Did she want this life for her unborn child? She knew at this point being with Dmitri was questionable. She had not told him about the baby maybe because in her subconscious she knew that she could not really be with him. Maybe she hesitated because she knew in her heart that Dmitri and her would never work.

"Who's child is it mine or Thompson?" Dmitri asked again, his eyes were red and he looked tired and exhausted. June knew then that this man would only make her life hell.

'It's not yours.' She said softly. Her admission came out like a breeze. The air froze as silence followed her words.

'June we are talking about a baby here, my heir.' Dmitri said after a few minutes.

She shook her head, 'You were right, I could not choose between you two and you were this billionaire who excited me and he was this stable down to earth guy who made me laugh.' she closed her eyes unable to look him in the face.

She reopened her eyes to see him standing up looking at her, his shoulders drooped.

His body defeated.

"So you ran from my bed to his? All this pristine white image was just one for show,' he was mad, she could she the various stages of comprehension dawn on his face, he felt slighted, ' Is that the way it's going to be? You pretend to everyone that you're this great person but instead you're a slut!"

She stood up and slapped him then, 'I am not and you know it! Gared is a wonderful guy, he cares for me, I wish he was my first, I wish I had waited for him instead I threw it away on you!'

There was utter silence for the second time in her apartment after her outburst. Dmitri's face was devoid of emotion now. He was looking at her like she was a stranger.

"Gared cares about me, he has been up front with me from the first time we met and he is just so gentle and so considerate." she added indeed Gared was all of these things.

A changed look came over Dmitri, "So you were playing with me, enjoying time with the rich bully."

"Gared is a real man, he is going to be a great father, something you will never be. It takes trust to build a relationship Dmitri trust and love something you are not capable of giving because you are just too obsessed with your work and controlling everyone else around you!" She said as she walked away from him.

Dmitri's face clouded over as he stared at her, her phone rang breaking the tension filled atmosphere. Dmitri picked up her phone which was on the sofa next to her bag. He looked at it his face contorting in rage as he clenched his jaw.

Dmitri held it up to her as Gared's name flashed on the screen. Dmitri placed the phone in her hands and walked to the door silently.

He stopped on the threshold and turned to stare at her piercingly with a deadly gaze and in the calmest voice possible he stated, 'I hope you never regret the choice you have made today, June. I loved you and you betrayed me. I don't forgive easily."

The raw emotion was so evident in his voice. Dmitri opened the door and walked away not looking back.

A/N: Please tell me what you think will happen?

Will she run after him?

Will Dmitri come back?

Why do you think Gared was calling?

Chapter 17

------

3 00 reads....Thank you to every one who reads and votes for my story ....Thank you, muchos gracias, merci, arigato, gamsahabnida, danke!

"Hello?" June said breathlessly.

"June, are you okay?" came Gared's concerned voice.

"I am fine, Gared." She answered a bit shaken trying to balance her shopping bags and her phone. She manoeuvred her way to the nearest bench in the shopping centre and sat.

"I called your office and they said you had the day off." Gared continued.

"Yes, May dragged me to go baby shopping since she will be going to Paris next week for a few months and wanted to buy me the latest baby wear before she left." June looked across at her sister who was glaring at her.

"I can only imagine the look she is giving you at the moment." Gared said laughingly as June joined his joke. May was still glaring at her and signed for her to end the call.

"You know her too well Gared; she will probably give you her death treatment when you next meet." May almost pulled the phone from her at that moment. "Gared I must say bye or else I'm chopped liver!"

"Please we need to keep these babies away from May's stares! I'll email you the Bernado documents and make an appointment with your administrator to see you sometime next week then. Give May my love!" He rang off in good humour.

"Bye Gared." June ended the call and May was quick to interrupt

"That man is impossible; he is so inconsiderate and clueless. If you are not at work why is he calling you on your personal mobile?" May complained and plopped herself on the bench beside June.

Gared had been working with her on a new project. Her new client had assigned him as their representative and they had been in close contact for the last two months. May had taken an instant dislike to Gared when she had met him at her office the first time. The two of them had been hurling insults back and forth ever since. Gared was usually so laid back but when May was around he was prickly and hot tempered. May being the trouble maker that she is riled him up even more.

"Sis I'm tired, my feet are swollen and my back is starting to throb." June looked at her ankles. They had swelled over her plimsolls. She needed to end this shopping trip before she collapsed. May was like a military colonel once she starts shopping she grills every sales assistant on the floor about a purchase to ensure that the style was designed perfectly. June did not know why she had agreed to go. Her hormones had made her too compassionate.

"Okay I guess we have enough stuff for now." May commented looking at the collection of bags that surrounded them on the bench. May gave her hand to her sister to help her up. June gladly accepted pulling her six month belly to a standing position. She felt like a whale and walked like one too.

"I can't carry anything, you did not think this through." June complained wanting to sit back down.

"I've got this sis." May reassured her as she called someone on her phone. A few minutes later a tall chauffeur appeared and he carried most of their bags to the awaiting SUV with May.

"See I do think of everything." May boasted as June settled in the soft interior of the vehicle. She needed a good foot rub and a jar of peanut butter. She had the worst craving for anything peanut.

June sat on the sofa her feet soaking in her home spa in her living room. May was unpacking the stuff they had bought in her bedroom which was also her nursery. She wanted her son close to her. June rubbed her stomach; the scan had revealed that she was going to have a son. she remembered that day so clearly.

The doctor turned to her and said, "You have very healthy and active baby Ms. Stapleton."

June could see the baby moving and stretching his legs."Indeed Dr. Montgomery, he moves all the time especially when it's time for meals.' the doctor laughed and told her to look closely at the screen.

'What am I looking for?' June was lost as she stared at her child doing aerobics and felt it as well.

The doctor pointed to the baby's lower body and said, 'As you can clearly see, you are having a boy!'

June stared at the body part which visibly showed that she was carrying a son.

"A boy", she murmured, 'a boy who would be strong and virile like his father.' She said distractedly, covering her mouth once she had uttered the words. She had often thought of Dmitri but she knew this was for the best she would have a better life without him; she would have to explain to her son about his father later on but with so much support from family and friends she was not worried about that as yet. She did not want her son to miss out greatly and she would tell Dmitri she just had not decided on a specific date.

"You okay June?" the doctor as concerned.

She realised that she was crying, 'I don't know what came over me, I am so happy, a boy." she countered feeling very emotional.

'It's okay June emotions are uncontrollable at this time,' she continued, 'for now everything looks fine, a few more months and he will be in your arms."

June was crying heavily now as the tears rolled down her cheeks, her son; hers and Dmitri, she took a deep breath, and they were going to have a son. She had left the doctor's office drained from her emotional upheaval. She had to share the news with Dmitri but how was she to do it after the way he had left.

Her parents had been eagerly awaiting to know the sex of the baby and had called when she had exited the doctor's surgery.

"Hello" she answered.

"Boy or girl?" asked her curious mother sounding excited on the phone.

"A boy mom." she responded happily and could hear her father on speakerphone shouting. "Get in there! Yeah, football, here we come!"

"No dad he will choose whatever sport he wants."

Her father was not listening as her parents totally ignored her and started to rant about things they would do with their grandchild.

"Mom, dad, enough already." June tried to calm her parents down.

"Sorry dear just got carried away."

'I'll say," she added with good humour.

She did not want to think of Dmitri. He was the past. June did not want to regret letting him go but it was for the best for now. At least that was what she convinced herself to think every day. Her life had been very peaceful since he left. The project in Sicily was finished and Jay would be back next week. Jay had nothing but glowing reports about working with Dmitri and that made her a bit annoyed but at least he was nice to Jay. She knew that the project had been a success and Jay was sure to get a promotion because of this. He deserved it since he had worked so well on his own.

"Hey J, you ready to eat?" May asked interrupting her reverie.

"Always." June replied as she laid her head back on the sofa.

Her parents had not been happy when she had told them about Dmitri's departure.

They had not been aware of her duplicity until then.

"June I will not support you raising this baby alone." Her mother was saying angrily after a family dinner.

April interjected, "Maybe there was a good reason for Dmitri leaving."

"Was there June, did he abandon you or did you not tell him about the pregnancy?" her mother asked very annoyed.

"Well, it's a bit complicated," June started, "Dmitri believes the baby is not his."

"No way!" shouted May, "The bastard!"

"Language May," her father reprimanded, "Why would he think that June?"

"Well there was this guy I dated for a while and Dmitri had me followed and this guy kissed me when I told him that there was no future for us and well Dmitri thinks the baby is not his!"

Everyone was staring at her in shock until her mother asked, "You led him to believe that didn't you June!"

June opened her mouth to object but she could not lie to her family. She nodded her head in agreement.

"June I am so disappointed in you, you need to correct this and tell Dmitri that he is going to be a father!" her mother was adamant.

"J I can't believe you did this! Dmitri must be in bits because he feels you betrayed him. The man was head over heels in love with you why would you sabotage that?" May came to her and held her hands. June felt like an egg. She was wrong, very very wrong.

"June you will call Dmitri and explain everything tonight."

"Mom, I can't." June was sobbing, "I can't." she said as she ran from the dining room to the bathroom.

She felt wretched inside knowing that she had made the wrong decision but she just wanted to hurt him but this had gone too far. She was in a dilemma. Her baby would grow up without a father and she could give it everything but not a father's love.

She could survive without Dmitri, she had for 25 years but her child should not.

She had convinced her family that she would tell Dmitri before the birth. May had threatened to call Dmitri if she did not. She knew that her family would definitely do so.

June stood in front of the mirror. Her breasts were full and ripe. Her stomach was huge and she felt like a whale most times. Her hair was longer and all her friends told her that pregnancy agreed with her. Indeed it was, she had practically bought everything for the baby. She wanted to work until the last minute and would take all her leave after the birth.

June had to go on with her life and decided retail therapy would be best to soothe her emotional state. It was Saturday and she decided to get a cab to visit an up scale baby store, in the Knightsbridge, Central London. There was an adorable navy blue jumper and shoes that she had seen there a few weeks ago. Now she new the baby's sex she would buy it if it was still for sale.

She got out of the cab and paid the driver. As she turned round she felt someone looking at her. Sure enough Dmitri stood across the street glaring at her rudely. The cab pulled away and his eyes widened as he took in her swollen belly. Franco also saw her and gave her a wry smile. They turned away sharply and entered the building behind him. June stood there on the pavement for a few moments trying to compose herself. The shock was too much.

'Lady are you alright?' a woman asked her nicely.

'Yes- yes' she stumbled; 'I'm fine now.' she smiled and continued on her way.

June would never forget the look in Dmitri's eyes as he assessed her. It was not pleasant or kind, far from it, it was filled with loath and hate. She numbly carried on with her shopping trying to forget the father of her unborn child.

That incident had been on her mind all week. Dmitri had been due in the office but luckily she had not seen him, just knowing that he was back made her uneasy.

"I am famished." June commented as she waited for the lift with Gared. They had just concluded a meeting and Gared had kindly invited her to have lunch with him.

"Ooh!" she said as her son turned around.

"Are you okay?" Gared asked concerned

"Yeah the little one is probably hungry as well he just moved." June responded smiling and holding her stomach as her son continued his acrobatics.

"Can I feel him?" Gared asked looking at her in awe.

"Sure." She agreed and took his hand to the spot where her son was practising some gymnastic move. Gared smiled as he felt his first kick.

"Awesome, he will definitely play football." Gared said after he felt another flutter.

"You are worse than my dad!" she chided him as the lift doors opened.

"June!" she looked up and saw Jay exiting the lift. He stood back and looked at her.

"You look amazing June!" he said before giving her a hug.

"Thanks, your tan is great!" she noticed that his skin had an olive glow to it now.

"Yeah, thanks." Jay was looking at Gared and June quizzically.

"Jay this is Gared Thompson, Jay is one of my colleagues who was away on assignment." the two men shook hands and greeted each other.

"We must catch up when I get back from lunch because I'm really hungry." She said stepping away from him.

"This little fella needs to be nourished." Gared said as he put his hand on her stomach again.

"See you later June." Jay said walking away.

"Bye." they said in unison.

The lift doors opened once again and June stilled. Dmitri stood in there his face turned to a stony mask as he looked at her. Gared's hand was still on her stomach.

"June! June?" Gared was looking at her.

"Oh!" she said stepping into the lift. Gared had a hand on her lower back as he guided her in.

"Ms Stapleton." Dmitri greeted as she stood in front of him.

June turned around slowly and greeted him firmly "Mr. Kanaredes, Franco." Franco was with him and he looked a bit uncomfortable shifting his feet and unable to meet her eyes.

Gared turned around and also greeted Dmitri.

"Ah Mr. Kanaredes, we met sometime earlier?" Gared prompted.

"Yes we did, remind me of your name again?" Dmitri was blunt as he acknowledged Gared.

"Gared Thompson." They shook hands. June closed her eyes and begged for freedom.

The ride was spent in silence and seemed to go on for an eternity. They got off the lift first and were walking toward the front entrance. June was aware of Dmitri following them. Gared's hand on the small of her back as well as holding her bag which really made them look like a couple.

Once outside Dmitri and Franco swiftly passed them walking towards a black Audi MPV.

Gared hailed a cab and got her in it and they left for lunch. June was an emotional wreck; seeing Dmitri again was hard. She felt like a fraud. She touched her stomach and closed her eyes trying to get Dmitri's glare out of her mind.

Chapter 18

As her due date approached June was filled with a sense of longing. Her sisters May and April had been too busy to be her birthing partner so Gared had volunteered. May had to go to France and April was doing her final exams of law school. Gared had been a real trooper especially when she revealed to him who her baby's father was, he had been shocked at first but had encouraged her to tell Dmitri like everyone else. However he understood her feelings and reluctance to tell Dmitri since he had met the man himself.

Similarly, her parents had put extreme pressure on her to tell Dmitri about the baby as well. Her mother although supportive had not been pleased that Dmitri was still unaware of his child's impending birth. June knew she was being a coward but also selfish. However she was afraid to tell Dmitri the truth now. How would he react? What would he do? Would he take her child away because he was angry? This fear prevented her from telling him anything.

Consequently by the time she reached her eighth month her duplicity gnawed at her. Dmitri was in London and after Jay told her that he had stopped by the office June knew that she had to confront him. It was her last chance to come clean. Dmitri had a right to know even if he would be angry at first he should know that he was going to be a father.

June finally called him to arrange a meeting face to face. Maybe seeing her would soften his anger which she knew would surface but she was ready. Franco had sounded wary on the phone but after consulting his boss she had been granted a few minutes with her child's father. June had insisted the meeting be held at her home not wanting any drama at his office. Dmitri had been stubborn and they had finally agreed for her to visit his home. The baby was low and walking was now a chore but she finally caved realising that this was her final chance to be honest with Dmitri.

She had been on maternity leave for the past three weeks and had barely left her house. She took a cab to his Belgravia home. She read the text he had sent her earlier.

I can only give you ten minutes.

Dmitri had been cold in his message, no greeting, no names, just a simple commanding statement. June was a bit rattled by his tone but she swallowed it because what she was about to do was worse. Since this was the first direct communication they had between them and not through Franco at least he was willing to meet her some way not quite half but some. She did not blame him, over the last few months their interactions had been non existent. Dmitri had not acknowledged her when they would meet at her workplace; he would stare at her growing belly and the fire would blaze in his eyes. So many times June had wanted to shout out the truth but she held back each time. Today she was going to do it.

June rang the doorbell of the opulent house. A maid she had not seen before opened the door and guided her to wait in one of the reception rooms. She was standing near the windows looking out at the well-manicured back garden, the roses were lovely all neatly blossoming in vibrant colours.

"June." Dmitri said from behind her. She turned around in her a double layer black swing maxi dress which swished with her movement. Dmitri stared at her piercingly. His expression was stony and hard but he still looked dashing in a brown pair of trousers and beige v neck jumper with a white shirt.

"Hi" June said softly her feet barely able to stand anymore. She had been in discomfort all morning but lately that had been the theme of her days. She rubbed her stomach as it felt heavier and heavier.

Slow down little one she mentally cooed to her unborn child as he was pushing against her already painful stomach.

Her back was really hurting. She needed to sit down.

"Can I sit?" She held her back and navigated her way to the nearest sofa. "My feet are killing me." He gestured to the beige sofa near the window. June sat down but with great difficulty.

Dmitri almost went to her as her face contorted in pain as she sat down but he held back.

"What do you want?" he asked impatient to know why she had asked to meet with him.

Dmitri looked at June and his heart constricted. She had to be the most beautiful pregnant woman he had ever seen. Her skin was glowing and her face was absolutely radiant. Her stomach was huge but she carried herself well. He put his hands in his pockets fisting them to regain some semblance of control. June had no idea the effect she had on him. He had fallen in love with her and her betrayal had shattered his heart. No woman had ever had such an effect on him and the one time he had let himself be normal that woman had betrayed him. He looked at her resplendent with another man's child growing inside her.

If only things had been different, he had had such plans for them. He had wanted her to be his forever from the first time they had met in his bedroom in the cottage. She had looked at his nakedness and the blush which had flushed her entire body had twisted his gut. She had looked so innocent and bewildered. Then her feisty attitude in always trying to defy him had sealed his love for her.

Even after she had let another man into her bed he tried to forgive her maybe there was a slim chance the child was his; so he had continued to follow her but seeing pictures of Gared Thompson taking her to lamaze classes, lunch, shopping for baby clothes and even accompanying her to doctor's visits on numerous occasions, he had finally accepted that June was not carrying his child.

He had concluded that Thompson was indeed the father. The man was devoted.

He had painfully let her go and pushed her out of his life by ignoring her. Now she wanted to see him and although he had wanted to deny her request he was curious as to what she wanted to say to him.

"What do you want June?" he asked again sounding bored.

"Dmitri you see," June paused and flexed her back as she was in great pain. "Sorry it's just that well ...my back is so painful could you put cushion behind me please?"

Dmitri shook his head in astonishment this woman had no limits!

He walked over and arranged a cushion behind her. She wriggled a bit and moaned. Dmitri went to the drinks cabinet, he needed a distraction.

"Do you want something to drink?" he asked avoiding to look at her as he opened a bottle of whiskey.

"I would love some apple juice and um, well you see...." She paused and said sheepishly, "and another cushion please?"

Dmitri looked at June, she was grimacing, although he was angry with her he could not stop himself from helping her.

"Are you okay June?" Dmitri was concerned since she looked like she was in great discomfort.

"I'm fine just a bit of back ache which is completely normal at this stage in my pregnancy." She smiled or contorted her face, he wasn't sure but she looked very, very uncomfortable.

He handed her the juice as he arranged another cushion for her however she drank a sip of the juice and scrunched her nose then handed it back to him. "Sorry but it can't go down."

This woman was trying his patience. He put the juice back on the trolley, maybe being angry was the best way to go.

"June just say what you need to and leave I have another appointment shortly." He walked to the glass doors moving further away from her.

"Fine, you see my parents feel that I treated you unfairly but..."

"I agree." Dmitri interrupted.

"I think we just had a huge misunderstanding over everything." June rambled. "We wanted different things from our relationship."

"June just say what you need." Dmitri cut in again firmly. He did not want to rehash the past.

"I want to say that I'm sorry for hurting you but you made me feel so constricted and I was not sure what would become of us..." June was feeling really unwell. She was starting to sweat and stopped what she was saying as her body began to tighten.

"June, I have another commitment in a few minutes, I only allowed this meeting because I thought you had something else to tell me." Dmitri knew that he had to send her away soon.

" If you came to apologise, I do not want to hear it. What you did doesn't deserve forgiveness and I never forgive betrayal."

June shifted her body as she felt a sharp pain in her lower back. She barely heard what Dmitri was saying; she shimmied her way to the edge of the sofa and held the arm rest.

"I think I need to use the toilet." She asked softly feeling like her bladder was going to burst.

As she tried to negotiate her body to get upright, Dmitri appeared and assisted her. She smiled at him in gratitude as her body felt tighter and tighter.

"Fine, follow me." Dmitri conceded as he looked at June and shook his head, she looked really uncomfortable and he led the way hoping she did not let go on his floors. His sister Eva, had wanted to use the toilet every five minutes when she was pregnant.

"Dmitri?" June asked from behind him.

What did she want now? He thought.

He turned around ready to scold her but she was leaning against the doorway and there was a pool of water streaming down her legs. He rushed to her; she was breathing very fast and holding her stomach.

"June you had an accident I will call Hilda." She held onto his arm to detain him.

"My. Water. Just. Broke. "She uttered between haggard breaths.

"Your what?!" Dmitri looked at June in shock. Her water! Her water! He thought over and over again.

He froze.

"Call. The. Ambulance." She was saying but he was far away. She was having her baby here in his house.

"Dmitri!" June screamed at him and he looked at her. Her face was aglow with sweat but she still looked so angelical. He assisted her back to the sofa before he called the ambulance. Then he called his PA.

"Franco." He barked into his phone a short while later, "Call June's family and tell them she is in labour and meet us at the hospital."

June was in the first stages of labour according to the paramedics and she had appeared to be in so much pain so that he had accompanied her with no hesitation. She may have hurt him but he could not hate her in this state. He held onto her hand as she breathed in ragged spurts and every now and then, she screamed out loudly. The pain appeared to be intense. He tried to comfort her as she struggled with her contractions.

"June you are going to be okay." He reassured her as she screamed through another contraction gripping his hand so tightly that her finger nails would dig into his skin. He could only grimace as she appeared to be in more agony than him.

"Dmitri, I need to tell you something ... " June was saying but Dmitri silenced her when he saw blood oozing down her legs.

He opened his eyes in shock. "She is bleeding? Is that normal?" he asked the paramedic who was checking the machines.

The paramedic lifted June's dress and examined her briefly and then looked at him.

"Sir, it is the next stage, it is the mucus plug or show which means the cervix is now unblocked, ready for the baby to come through."

Dmitri was amazed. He looked at June who was breathing a bit normally now but still holding onto him tightly.

"She will be fine." The female paramedic said with a smile. " The expectant fathers seem to worry more than the mothers."

"I'm n....." He was cut off as a wave of pain flashed through June's face and she screamed out again.

"Please Dmitri I need to say that --" June was trying to tell Dmitri the truth but he put a finger to her lips.

"No need to say anything, just be calm so you can have a healthy baby." Dmitri stopped her and kept holding her hand as her contractions zipped through her body. She was determined to tell him the truth even more now but they soon arrived at the hospital and she was wheeled into a labour room.

Dmitri had made Franco arrange for her to be put in the private maternity ward at Chelsea and Westminster Hospital. June was oblivious to all this as she was led to Kensington Wing in the hospital. The medical staff attending to her were busy connecting her to wires as she grappled with her labour pains. Dmitri had not left her side.

"Dmitri," June was saying. "I need to tell you something."

She screamed as a contraction came on.

"June just concentrate on having this baby whatever you want to tell me wait after the birth."

"But..."

"Please June," he begged as the doctor entered the room.

"Hi I'm Dr Pascal." The short bald man told her as he examined her intimately.

"You are dilating very quickly, you're 8 cm dilated right now, things are moving well." The doctor stated before leaving the room.

"Don't you want something to reduce the pain?" one of the nurses asked her.

"No drugs just some gas and air." She said determinedly. The nurses began to prepare the machine and showed them how to use the mask. June would inhale the gaseous mixture when she felt she needed it.

"Is it safe ?" Dmitri asked puzzled at this form of pain relief.

"It is totally harmless and will not affect your wife or baby at all." one of the nurses replied.

His phone buzzed before he could correct the nurse.

"Franco what is the update?" He asked his PA as June sucked in some more gas.

"The Stapletons are on their way to the ward. I sent someone to pick them up as you instructed. They should be arriving shortly." His ever efficient PA informed him smoothly.

"Great and thanks." He responded ending the call.

"Your family will be arriving very soon." He told June, she smiled at him.

"Dmitri, thank you but I really need to tell you what I came to see you about today." She looked at her stomach and sighed. "I wanted to do this before the baby is born, I'm so sorry for hurting you, I never meant to."

"June concentrate on having this baby first." She shook her head at him.

"Please listen, you see this baby is--"

"June!" came a sound from the doorway.

It was June's mother who rushed in followed by her dad.

Her mother rushed to hug her daughter.

"My baby is having a baby." Her mother said lovingly. "How are you doing? Are you handling the pain well?"

June smiled "It hurts like nothing I have ever felt before but I'm coping."

"My strong and brave girl." Her dad came forward.

"How are you my princess?" they hugged her.

"I'm okay Daddy." June looked over to him.

"Dmitri has been wonderful through all this." She praised him as her mother came over to hug him as well.

"Oh my, I'm so happy you are here." She looked at Dmitri her face alive. "You see I told you he would understand." Mrs Stapleton hugged him again. He offered her his chair beside June as he went to shake hands with her father.

"Thanks for everything; I'm happy you have forgiven her. I was a bit disappointed with the whole situation but it's good to see you at her side. Forgiveness is a good thing." Dmitri nodded at the older man a bit confused.

Is that what June wanted to tell him? She wanted him to forgive her? Did she want peace before having her child?

Franco sent him a message and he excused himself from the room.

"We understand." June's mother told him. "Settle these issues now because soon you won't have the time when June delivers."

Dmitri met Franco outside.

"Sir the rest of the family is coming up including Mr Thompson."

Dmitri cringed at the name. He should not be surprised since any father would want to be there to see his child born. He had forgotten that June was not having his child for a minute. He had to take control of himself. He was no longer needed. He should not even be here.

"Dmitri!" he turned to be enveloped into a hug by May Stapleton.

"Hi" he responded as she stepped back.

"I'm so happy you are here, I was so shocked when Mom told me that you were with J. Thanks for forgiving her." May told him and he smiled weakly. How is she?

"In a lot of pain but she is handling it superbly." He had felt proud of June in the way she was dealing with labour. "It is obviously very painful but she is doing brilliantly."

"That's my sis." He let her go in to visit her sister and soon April came running in.

"Oh Dmitri so happy you are here?" she also hugged him. "You and my sis all good now?" she asked hesitantly.

"Yeah!" he said not wanting to explore his feelings for June again.

"Whew.... we knew she was wrong but so happy that it ended well for both of you." April also rushed in.

"How is she doing?" he asked a nurse who was leaving the room.

"She is 10 cm dilated so we are going to begin delivery soon." The nurse told him walking away.

"Mr Kanaredes, what are you doing here?" Dmitri stilled as Gared approached him.

Chapter 19

"He is adorable!" June's Mom cooed rocking her newborn grandson in her arms. "His skin is so soft." She continued as she rubbed her finger across his cheek.

"Dear, pass him along there is a queue here!" her dad eagerly stretched out his hands and her mother reluctantly deposited the sleeping baby into his grandfather's arms.

"He feels so heavy, aww." Her dad looked overwhelmed his eyes transfixed on the baby held in his arms who was fast asleep after coming into this world a few hours ago.

"The two of you are hogging and will definitely spoil him." May complained laughingly as she encouraged April to support her.

"You already held him, plus it is our duty as grandparents." Her mother countered.

Her son weighed 8lbs 10 ozs; he had a full head of dark hair, long limbs and the same patrician nose as his father. He would be tall and handsome, so far the only thing of hers he had were her blue eyes.

June groggily shifted on her bed. The delivery had been real tough. She had gone in for a normal delivery with no complications but suddenly while in the delivery room her son's heart rate was falling quickly. The doctor had listed her as critical and almost cancelled the normal delivery to turn it into a caesarean. Luckily her son was eager and rushed out. June then lost a lot of blood in the process, her blood pressure rose dangerously high and she slipped into a coma. She had to have blood given to her. However things took a turn for the better and she woke up. She had just held her son for the first time an hour earlier five hours after he was born.

She looked at her family cooing and gushing over her son she was so relieved that it was all over. She was very sore but extremely ecstatic she s had her son.

"It is feeding time!" a nurse walked into the room and took the baby from his grandfather.

"I'm not used to this as yet." June commented from her hospital bed. She was tired but just holding her son made her feel so refreshed. The nurse arranged her son in her arms and guided her on feeding him.

"That is it, let him suckle and get accustomed to the action." The nurse ensured that her son's head was correctly positioned.

"It feels weird; I can feel the fluid move." June was stating about the breast-feeding.

"That is a good sign; it seems your milk has come in early." The nurse said as she stood back after ensuring that June could continue on her own.

"Let him suck as much as he wants on the breast, to help him get used to the motion and also to aid your body to produce milk." June was amazed at her son. His mouth was tightly latched to her breast and he was suckling quite well.

"You both seem to have caught on pretty quickly. I will leave you to it then. Call the nurses station if you need any further assistance."

"Thanks." June said smirking as the nurse left her room.

He appeared hungry and after 10 minutes she was unsure if she should stop him as he continued to suck. His eyes were closing and she was unsure what to do.

"He has been feeding for a while, should I stop?" June looked up at her mother who was seated on the foot of her bed.

"No keep on for about 20 minutes and see," her mother advised her.

Her son was sleeping soundly after being fed ten minutes ago. Breastfeeding had felt strange at first but the sensation was filled with pride as her son suckled from her. His small eyes were open and bright. She knew she would love him for life.

"So June what name have you decided for this precious one?" her mother asked.

"Jonathan Zack Stapleton," she said confidently.

"Ooh that is beautiful J!" May complimented.

"A fitting tribute my girl," her father gave her a hug. Jonathan was her paternal grandfather's name and Zack was her maternal grandfather's name.

"Great choice, he certainly looks like a Jonathan." April added looking pleased.

"Stapleton?" her mother inquired looking at her. "No tribute to his real father?"

"Mom, I don't want to discuss this!" June said annoyed.

"Honey, what about his father? What happened to you and Dmitri?" her mother was prodding

"Mom, J needs to rest." April tried to divert the elephant in the room.

"No, we are going to discuss this, my grandson will not be raised like this!" her mother was not going to end this.

"Dear, June has had a rough day, she needs to rest we can talk about this another day." Her father tried to pacify the situation.

However her mother was out for blood.

"Mom let her rest." May tried to collect their bags.

"No, June why did he leave? He was here why did he go" her mother was adamant on this and this made June realise that she had to at least pacify her family. Dmitri had disappeared during her delivery. She guessed he had seen Gared and decided to leave. She did not have the heart to tell her family that she lost the opportunity to tell Dmitri about their son. Her mother would be livid.

"June, try to rest, we will see you tomorrow." April gave her a hug and a kiss as she tried to guide her mother out of the room.

"I am not going to be silenced here. June I want answers!" her mother insisted.

"Let her rest, dear, we will discuss this later." Her dad gave her a kiss

"Fine but we need to talk seriously, okay June?" her mother finally relented as she was ushered out of the room.

June lay back and watched her son's chest moving up and down. She walked over to him and touched his chubby cheek. He really was a picture of Dmitri. Gared had been supportive and he had been very helpful. He had stayed until she had woken up but he knew it was not his place to stay around.

No one really knew when Dmitri had left. It seems that while June was being taken to the delivery room Dmitri had just disappeared. June wondered where he was when she awoke but May had told her that he had left while she was in the delivery room. She held nothing against him and she was at least grateful to him for being there when she had gone into labour.

She knew that telling Dmitri about their son now would be catastrophic but maybe it was not meant to be. She knew that he needed to know but somehow the time had never been right and the opportunity had never clearly presented itself.

June returned to work three months later on a part time basis. She didn't want to leave little Zack alone for too long. Gared was his godfather and her two sisters doubled up as godmothers. Zack was spoiled and fussed over. She had gone into consultancy work in order to devote more time to motherhood. Mr. Hamilton was loathing losing her so he was agreeable to let her choose her work pattern.

She mostly worked from home and only went to the office for meetings or reviews.

Her son was growing rapidly; he was a good baby and had a great appetite again. It was remarkable how strong Dmitri's genes were. She saw him in all of Zack's movements. She had not seen Dmitri at the office and since the business project with his company was over he no longer had a cause to be in their building. There was absolutely no news from him or of him. He had always been a private person so the media had no information about him. She had spotted an article about him in Forbes magazine but his interview had been squarely focused on his business with nothing about him personally or his private life.

It was a normal Wednesday morning and June was eager to finish this assignment when her boss told her that he wanted to see her.

'Please have a seat, June.' Mr. Hamilton gestured as she entered his office.

She sat wondering what was up.

'The Elberg account has been going well but I want you to over the final overview, personally.' Mr. Hamilton said brightly.

The Elberg report was stationed in New York. June looked panicked at her boss.

'Sir, you want me to go to New York?' June asked to confirm her thoughts.

'Yes only for a few days, they are hosting a gala event to promote the new convention centre and they want you present at the opening ceremony." Mr Hamilton stated looking very proud.

'A few days?' June said amazed; she had never spent a day away from Zack since his birth eleven months ago. A few hours but a few days?

'I know that you don't want to be away from your son, June but its only for a short time and I need you to take this over, Jay is in the Bahamas and Minoa is in Athens," she looked at her boss trying to digest his words, " You carried this project and you deserve to be there. I am so proud of you since you are juggling motherhood and work and still giving me excellent results."

She knew this day would come but she had to face it now.

"I have never been away from my son for a day." She voiced openly thinking about her decision. She was proud of her work on the Elberg account. She had supervised it since it began before Zack's birth and now it was completed she happy it was her handiwork. Elberg and Associates had been quite pleased at her efficiency in ensuring that the project was completed and continued during her maternity leave. Although she had never seen the building in person the finished work was exemplary from the pictures she had seen. June did not know what to do. Zack was turning one next month but she was unsure.

"Sir can I give you my answer tomorrow?" June asked

"Sure we need to finalise the event by noon so I expect a response before then June." With that she was dismissed.

June went home pondering on her decision she had to make.

She called her sisters to come over to throw the idea at them.

Zack was being fed before settling him for the night.

He was busy throwing his food everywhere as usual except into his mouth. He loved food time and was messy but eventually ending up eating.

"Mama!" Zack squealed with delight as she placed his cup of milk in front of him.

"Hey you!" June responded ruffling his hair.

"Mama!" he squealed again.

She mimicked putting a spoon into her mouth as he remembered what he was doing and continued eating.

"You are doing so well." She cooed as he had eaten most of the food on his plate.

"Ooh, Ooh!" Zack giggled continuing to feed himself happy with her compliment.

The doorbell rang and she went to answer it. It was her sisters.

"Hi J!" May greeted giving her a hug and rushing to Zack in his chair.

"Hello Sis." April said also giving her a hug and also going over to Zack.

He was laughing excitedly at the sight of his aunts knowing that they would spoil him tonight.

"My big boy, how are you?" May greeted and Zack opened his arms to give her a messy hug. He dropped his spoon on the floor as he was so delighted.

"Move over," April said getting in the action.

"Ahh ahh! Mama!" Zack squealed as his aunts showered him with kisses and cuddles.

"Enough you two let the child eat his supper!" June intervened looking at her sisters all covered up in baby food.

Zack was busily feeding May and April who in turn made him spoon some food into his mouth. June took the opportunity to prepare her son's bath.

An hour later her son was sleeping soundly in his room. His soft snores could be heard on the baby monitor she had in the living area. June had moved into a maisonette three months ago. Her new home had three bedrooms and two bathrooms. The living area was an open plan reception room and kitchen. Although the space was one unit it was cleverly split into three distinct areas that she used as her living area, kitchen/ diner and play area for Zack. She now had a back garden where she set up a mini playground for Zack. He enjoyed playing on the grass and learning with his huge Lego blocks.

Gared had come over towards the end of Zack's bedtime routine. He had become a great confidante and friend. He was the only one who knew that she had never told Dmitri about Zack. Her family had assumed that Dmitri was not interested in being a father and had chosen to not be in his son's life.

"So what is the crisis that brought us here tonight?" May asked sitting Indian style on the sofa.

"My boss wants me to attend the opening of a convention centre I helped set up in New York." June stated sipping her glass of juice.

"New York?" May repeated stunned.

"You need to go J." April said openly. June looked at her younger sister.

"Really?" she asked in doubt.

"Definitely." agreed May, "What kind of event is it? Formal? Black Tie? Casual?"

"Black tie event,Elberg and Associates are New York top brass." June replied

"It will be a good opportunity for Zack to show his independence since he will soon be one." Gared added.

"You need to do this June and for once I agree with him!" May exclaimed giving Gared a dubious look, "It's New York and Zack can stay with us for the time you are away."

"Sure, you need the break from Zack," April raised her finger at June who wanted to interrupt, " Yes, he is your son we know but you have been constantly there, he needs to become less attached."

"No, I'm not leaving my son!" June was adamant.

"So you don't trust us?" May asked glaring at her sister. Before June could respond Gared spoke.

"April yes but you...hmm?" Gared added bending his head to one side to look at May with doubt. May threw a cushion at him which he caught and threw right back at her. It took her unawares and hit her smack dab on the face. May got up and threw two cushions in quick succession, the first flew past Gared and the second hit him on the head.

"You two behave, sit May and leave Gared alone!" June reprimanded. Gared and May were always fighting or disagreeing about something. May grudgingly sat down after giving Gared a death glare. Gared smiled at her wickedly and arranged the cushions at his back and lounged on them.

June looked at her sisters and her friend. She was stuck but she had a good family and friend network and maybe it was time to ease her maternal reins a little bit.

"Of course I trust you guys." She said quickly after making her decision. " I will go to New York."

"It is settled then, we baby sit our adorable nephew while you go to New York." May said with certainty.

"Well...." June was still thinking, "Okay but I have my list of ground rules." She added.

"I have the perfect dress for you!" May exclaimed loudly. "It is a new design I fashioned for a show last month in Milan and it would be perfect for your first post baby glamour appearance."

June wrung her fingers did she make the right choice? Zack would be fine but would she?

June hated leaving Zack but her sisters promised he would be okay with them and her parents would be there as well. She felt like her heart was being pulled out when she kissed him goodbye. He gave her one of his slurpy kisses and cooed. She loved her son so much.

On the plane ride she tried to concentrate n her work but it was tough.

She missed Zack already.

She called her parents as soon as she landed at La Guardia Airport.

They told her not to worry and she tried not to but that was like telling the sea to stop being salty. Her son cooed when he heard her voice on the speaker phone but he sounded happy and excited. June relaxed somewhat as she made her way to her hotel in Manhattan.

The dress May had picked out for her would arrive tomorrow afternoon. June hoped it fit as she had no other option. She had decided to shop for the rest of the day and tomorrow she would oversee the final preparation for the opening gala.

The next day June was up early as the time difference was five hours between New York and London. Her son had slept throughout the night like he had been doing since he was six months old. He was currently in the park with her parents enjoying the swings and the slide.

Zack had mastered a few steps and had loved to use his feet. She imagined him running around on the grass.

The morning was spent finalizing the evening's gala celebration. Her team had been very efficient and she had finished by 1 pm. She had booked a spa treatment with the works. She would do her hair, face and nails after getting a relaxing mud treatment.

It was nearly five pm when June got back to her hotel room. She carried her dress box into her room. It had been delivered while she was out. She laid the box on the bed and removed the lid. She opened the tissue wrapping and pulled out the red creation. It was absolutely gorgeous.

It was a red mermaid sheer lace dress with nude lining and a short sweep train; 3/4 sleeves and a scooped neckline. The back had a plunging sweep which exposed most of her back. There were silver ankle strap open toe stiletto heels and silver accessories to complete the look. June put on the dress and looked at herself in the mirror. She had not felt this sexy since giving birth. She had worked had to lose the baby weight and she was pleased with how he hips were curvy and her breasts look so much fuller. She let her hair fall in waves to the right side of her neck. She had lightened her red hair and loved the combination tones. It made her paler skin look more alive.

She took a picture and sent it through a text message to May to thank her for the dress.

Thanks so much for such a beautiful dress, sis.

You look absolutely amazing J!

I feel amazing, how is my boy?

Asleep, he is such a good boy, we took him to Aunt Celia's and he loved Uncle Ivan's beard. He kept trying to pull it off.

Oh my! I miss him so much.

Who would guess that from the 100 texts I received today on my phone from you? Surely you could have sent some more?

Behave, thanks again. I must dash, my cab just arrived. Bye!

Bye sis and enjoy!

June entered the ballroom to see that the party was just beginning.

Sergio the assistant who was assigned to her came running toward her. He was decked up in his tuxedo.

"Ah senorita bellísima, bellísima' he said admiringly in his thick Italian accent.

"Molten grazie," she responded with a little curtsy.

'Let's begin!" She moved to ensure that this evening would be perfect.

Guests were arriving all dressed fabulously. The staff were working brilliantly to ensure that everyone was fed and thirst quenched.

"Ms Stapleton" Mr Elberg said as she approached him. " You look ravishing and this event would not be possible without you."

"Thank you sir." He was a middle aged man with peppered grey hair and a Robert De Niro look.

"Meet my lovely wife Sophia." June shook hands with a blonde Barbie who looked like she was barely legal to drive. She was heavily made up and her ample chest courtesy of a cosmetic clinic was dangerously teetering to spill out of her gold dress. June gave a polite smile and quickly excused herself.

William Elberg took to the stage and the ceremony began. He gave a marvellous speech and the convention centre was formally unveiled by the Mayor of New York. The night continued with entertainment from a popular musical group.

June was pleased. She kept in the shadows not wanting to be sucked in the crowd. She had made her rounds early and had even exchanged a few personal business cards.

At the end of the presentation Mr Elberg came back onto the stage to give the final words.

"I would also like to thank a simply talented and hardworking young lady, who can multi-task very well. She single handedly ensured this building was completed on time and with a high standard of quality. She ensured this was done throughout her pregnancy and also after it. In addition, she achieved all of this from where she is based in London. Please assist me in welcoming Ms. June Stapleton to the stage."

June shook her head and mouthed 'no' but Sergio guided her onto the stage as the applause got louder, she reluctantly walked onto the small stage and bowed.

'Ladies and gentlemen, Ms. June Stapleton, a truly remarkable woman.' Mr Elberg continued. She smiled as he took her hand and she gave a small curtsy.

He handed her a plaque. She took the plaque which was shaped like a beacon with an inscription that said " May you continue to light the path where your feet touch".

"Thank you." June said nervously as she accepted it humbly.

As she turned to look at the crowd her eyes fell on a figure at the back of the room.

Dmitri stood there staring at her.

A design of June's dress above.

Chapter 20

June froze. Dmitri was staring at her with a real piercing stare. She quickly gained her composure and left the stage. She needed to leave as soon as it was possible. She had not seen or heard from him ever since Zack was born. He had just disappeared. She wondered why he had left without a goodbye but she knew that he probably felt like an outsider.

She was blindly walking away from where she had seen Dmitri when she collided with a hard chest. She stumbled back but strong arms supported her. She steadied herself on her stiletto heels.

'I'm so sorry.' she mumbled fixing her dress she looked at her rescuer and remained speechless it was

Dmitri, he gazed at her blandly, 'You need to be more careful June.'

He was even more handsome. He had grown a beard which suited him and made him look even more dashing. his tuxedo fitted him to perfection.

'The convention centre is well done.' Dmitri remarked.

She forced a smile, 'Just doing my job but thanks."

June was suffocating in his presence. She was lost being around him. he looked so dashing and guilt riddled her as well over Zack's paternity.

'I'm surprised you made the trip knowing your circumstances.' he drawled.

"It is business and sometimes it has to be done." she responded hoping to escape him.

"Ah Kanaredes, so pleased to have you here." Mr Elberg joined in shaking Dmitri's hand.

"You know he introduced me to your company and I'm pleased that it worked out." He turned to June smiling.

"Really?" June was shocked; Dmitri had actually looked for additional business for them.

"Indeed, I trust his business decisions greatly, we have had many successful partnerships over the years and this one is the latest in a long line of alliances." Elberg was revealing a lot. June was a bit stumped at Dmitri's power and business expertise.

"Oh wow that is wonderful." June stated watching Dmitri who was very quiet.

"So June, have you and Dmitri had a good catch up?" Mr Elberg looked back and forth between the two of them. He appeared to be reading something.

"June and I were just reacquainting ourselves. I have not seen her in almost a year." Dmitri supplied.

"Splendid, she is a real worker this one here and all the while, doing it as a single mother." June stilled at Elberg's revelation. She quickly glanced at Dmitri to see his reaction. Dmitri looked at her firmly his eyes widening slightly at Elberg's admission.

"Really? Your relationship with your child's father did not work out?" Dmitri said surprised. "What was his name again Fred?"

June did not know what to say she was caught out and also annoyed at Dmitri's tone when he mentioned Gared's name.

"Gared and I decided to remain as friends." She inserted hoping to move on and leave this horrible conversation. Dmitri stared at her; his brain appeared to be thinking about something.

Did Dmitri look smug? A glimmer of a smile played on his face but it was so quick she may have missed it.

"Oh my June, you are raising your son alone? I guess your choice was the wrong one." June wanted to scream. Dmitri was relishing this even if it was only partially the truth.

"Ah Kanaredes when will you settle down, have a bambino or two?" William patted him on the back. Dmitri smiled roughly.

"I guess when I find the right woman, a trustworthy and loyal one is hard to find." Dmitri had aimed straight for her heart and he had got his target.

"Kanaredes look at me, I found my jewel in Sophia, she makes this old man happy, and that is all that matters to me." William glanced at his wife whose jewels were indeed sparkling as she laughed and sashayed towards them.

June stifled a fake yawn.

"Oh my, my clock is still on British time, it is late and I do have a long flight back to London tomorrow." She was escaping and she did not care. "It was a pleasure working with you Mr Elberg." She gave him a firm handshake and turned to Dmitri, "It was nice to see you again Mr Kanaredes." She did not extend her hand.

"Excuse me and enjoy the rest of the evening." Elberg left to join his wife and by the pinch he gave to her arse, he was still a horny old toad.

She was heading for the exit after extending her goodbyes to the staff especially Sergio, when someone touched her arm. She turned around startled by the distraction.

"Excuse me Miss Stapleton but Mr. Kanaredes would like to offer you a lift as you both are guests at the same hotel." Franco stated

"Oh Franco, how have you been?" she asked genuinely concerned.

"He treating you well?" June asked playfully.

Franco gave a slight smile. "He is indeed and waiting in the car as we speak."

"Franco I would prefer to make my own way." She stated descending the stairs to get a cab.

"Ms Stapleton, it is quite late and taxicabs are not always safe at this time of the night." She turned around and looked at Franco, who looked genuinely worried for her welfare.

"I am only accepting the ride because of you." She said as she entered the black limo parked at the entrance.

Dmitri was quietly typing something on his tablet as she took a seat far away from him. Franco got in the front with the driver and they set off. June wanted to be rude but she quietly said,

"Thanks for the ride."

"You are welcome." Came the even quieter response.

June chose to send a text to May who was most likely the only one awake at this time. There was no response so she guessed she was asleep.

June was about to put her phone back into her purse when the car jerked as the driver made an emergency stop. She flew to the opposite side of the seat and straight into Dmitri's arms. He caught her and kept her cocooned in his embrace.

Franco put down the partition.

"Sorry Mr Kanaredes, there was an intoxicated pedestrian who decided to cross the road suddenly. Are you alright, sir? Ms Stapleton?"

"We are fine." Dmitri responded and put the partition back in place. June tried to extricate herself from his arms but he held her firmly.

"I am okay; you can let me go now." He let her go and picked up her purse and handed it to her.

"Thank you." She said moving furthest away from him again.

They soon arrived at the hotel to June's relief.

Dmitri escorted her to the lift. Franco did not follow them inside. June got in and tried to look away from Dmitri who was casually leaning against the lift while typing into his mobile.

"We're here." Dmitri said holding her hand and leading her to her room. She paused as she took in the surroundings. This was not her floor. She stopped and pulled her hand out of his grip.

"This is not my floor." She was making her way back to the lift but Dmitri picked her up and carried her to the solitary door on the floor which she guessed was the penthouse suite.

"Let me down Dmitri!" she said struggling to be released. He opened the door of the suite and walked with her into another room and deposited her on the bed. He lay down over her before she could make sense of what was happening.

"We both know this is how the night would end." He said before his lips captured hers. June wanted to fight him but as his tongue plundered her mouth the memories of their past coupling flooded back and she succumbed to him. She wound her arm around his neck and let her body feel the passion of Dmitri's touch. They made love all night. It was like they had been starving for each other. The more he gave the more she matched him. It was subliminal.

June was awakened by Dmitri prodding her. It was around dawn as she could see the filters of sunlight through the drapes. She did not want to fully open her eyes to face him. The consequences of letting him make love to her were slowly taking a heel in her head.

"You have an important call June. It's Gared." he said a bit angrily. June's eyes flew open.

June sat up instantly, pulling the sheet with her. She grabbed the mobile from Dmitri.

"Hello?" she said anxiously.

"Oh my goodness June, we have been trying to contact you all night!" Gared said in relief.

Dmitri got off the bed after glancing at her angrily. He walked naked into the bathroom. The man was too sexy; she got a bit wet just watching him. He grabbed a toothbrush and began the process to clean his teeth. June was watching him and could barely hear what Gared was saying.

"Zack?" she repeated coming back to focus on the conversation at hand.

"Yes Zack is in hospital, he is...."

"Hospital, what is wrong?" she screamed, her baby was sick."Did he get hurt? Does he have a fever?"

"June, calm down, he is undergoing some preliminary tests..."

"Wait! What? When did this happen, did he fall?" She was asking everything she thought could be the cause. Zack was never sick except for the normal viruses and vaccination reactions. He had been fine. Is it because she left him? Or? She looked at Dmitri; is she being punished for not telling him about their son?

"He had a fever which was not getting better so your parents took him to A&E." Gared continued to fill her in on the situation.

"A fever? Since when?" She was worried that this fever was something more sinister.

"Yesterday evening, we tried calling but you never picked up." Gared filled her in.

June felt wretched ... yesterday? Yesterday? She was a real bad mother. She had been busy enjoying herself sexually and her son was getting worse.

This really was punishment.

"June, June?" Gared was calling out her name.

"What is the diagnosis?" She asked her voice shaking.

"We don't know. The doctors are still carrying tests." Came the smooth response. Gared was being too vague and she did not like it. "Zack is stable but they are checking to find out what caused his fever."

"I'll take the first plane back, keep me updated. Oh my poor baby, Gared take care of him until I come back please do that for me!" she begged as tears descended freely.

"I will; just get yourself over here. I will keep you updated." he promised.

"Thanks Gared, give him a kiss for me, let him know I love him." She put the phone down and scrambled to find her clothes which were all over the floor.

Dmitri came to her as she tried to look for her clothes. He held her arms and made her stand up from being on her knees on the floor.

"What is wrong June?" he asked sounding so concerned.

"Zack he is in hospital, my baby is sick." She moaned as Dmitri enveloped her in his arms. She buried her face in his chest relishing the comforting arms that surrounded her.

"What's wrong?" Dmitri asked softly patting her hair.

"They don't know. Zack had a fever and my parents took him to the hospital. They are still doing tests." She got out of his arms. "I need to go. I need to get a flight." She was blindly collecting her strewn clothing.

She was grabbing her shoes when Dmitri took everything from her and pushed her toward the bathroom.

"Have a shower, let me organise this for you." He said reassuringly.

She looked at him broken, she opened her mouth to tell him about Zack but the words were stuck.

Dmitri wiped her tears, "Go on and have a shower, I'll arrange everything." He turned on the tap and pushed her into the cubicle.

In spite of everything he still loved her. He picked up his phone and dialled his PA.

"Franco get my private jet ready we need to go to London immediately."

"But sir the meeting with..."

"Cancel everything; Ms. Stapleton's son is in hospital. Get everything prepared for our journey to the UK." Dmitri was in awe. June appeared to be in a state of shock. Last night he had hoped to use her and make her feel like dirt but the sex had been unbelievable as usual and he was rethinking his revenge plan. Now this new development put his plan on serious hold. Ever since he had seen her at the party he had wanted her in his bed again. When he had found out she was no longer attached he knew he would get her in his arms again. Now he was going to help her because she needed the help.

June was in a daze as she exited the bathroom. An outfit was on the bed and she dressed and searched for her phone. It was not in her purse. Where could it be?

"Looking for this?" Dmitri who was fully dressed handed her, her mobile.

"Thanks. Where was it?" she asked as she unlocked it.

"The driver found it in the limo this morning."

She had many missed calls from her family and text messages. She called her mother who answered on the fifth ring.

"June are you okay?" Her mother asked worriedly.

"How is Zack?" she asked desperate for some good news.

"He is in with the doctors they are not letting us see him. They say they have to do tests."

"Tests? What kind of tests? I thought he just had a fever, Zack is never sick." June adamantly said.

"He is now asleep and the doctors are doing their best. He will be fine. Just be calm and get yourself over here." Her mother reassured her.

"I should never have left him." she started to cry again, "It is my entire fault. I'm getting punished for lying, oh my precious baby." June felt like falling apart, guilt gnawed at her heart and she felt like she was suffocating.

"Honey just be strong for your son, you need to be strong for Zack!" her mother encouraged.

"Oh Mom I feel so bad, what can I do? It will take ages to get there. Oh no, my baby needs me and I am not there." She was starting to hyperventilate. Dmitri took the phone from her and wrapped her in his arms.

"June try to breathe, that is it, breathe, take another deep breath, come on. You need to be a strong mother, your son needs that love." Dmitri was pushing her to be firm.

"Mrs Stapleton we are on our way, we will travel by my private jet and be there soon. Just take care of the little one until we get there."

"That is good to hear, I'm happy you are there, at least you can comfort each other, you must be worried as well." Her mother responded relief flooding her voice.

Dmitri ended the call a bit puzzled at Mrs Stapleton's statement; something June had said about lying also piqued his curiosity. He did not want to speculate. June needed him now.

June was restless on the plane she appeared so preoccupied as she was pacing. Dmitri tried to get June to sleep but she refused. She was either pacing or sitting and shifting every few minutes. Even Franco was frazzled by it. Everyone was on edge by her anxiety. they had kept regular updates on June's son but no concrete information had been released by the doctors.

"Mr Kanaredes, would you like some refreshments?" the stewardess asked politely.

"Yes some warm soup. Thank you." The stewardess went to prepare his meal as he had a shot of whiskey. He needed to calm himself as well. Something was bothering June more than her son's illness she would look at him and stare and then look like she wanted to tell him something and then change her mind.

The stewardess brought the soup and Dmitri went over to June. She had not eaten all day.

"Here have some soup." He instructed. June shook her head in response.

"June you need to eat to be strong. You can't be there for your son if you too are ill, now eat!" he said forcefully.

June looked out of the plane window. She was now curled up in the seat. Dmitri pulled her onto his lap and scooped up a spoon of soup.

"Open your mouth!" he commanded, June looked at him in shock but she opened her mouth slowly. He fed her the soup. "Now swallow, that is a good girl, open?"

Dmitri fed her the entire bowl of soup when she was done he held her until she fell asleep. He too nodded off after their antics last night he was feeling a bit tired as well.

"Sir? Sir? We are ready to land." He opened his eyes to Franco's voice. He nodded his head and glanced at the woman in his arms. Her eyes were open and she was awake but she had remained in his embrace. He smiled slightly, if only, he wondered; if Zack was his son instead of Thompson's.

He still wanted her and always would. She made him angry but it lit a fire within him which he never knew he had. He had always been impassive to romance but June Stapleton had awakened his sleeping heart and captured it. Although she had betrayed him, he could not let her go. He tried to disappear from her life but every time they met he knew he had to have her again. Maybe he could start over with her. She and Thompson were over, maybe Zack and June could be his family now. He tightened his embrace and she snuggled deeper.

They had arrived at the hospital. June flew out of the lift and rushed to where her family had gathered outside of the ICU.

She ran straight into her mother's arms.

"Oh mom how is he? I need to see him." She demanded eagerly.

"Zack is in a medically induced coma." Her mother informed her. "Honey the doctor is in there right now, when he comes out we will know something."

June went to the door and she peeked in and saw her son connected to many wires. His tiny body looked so desolate on the bed. She could not lose him. He was her everything. The doctor came out with some nurses from Zack's room.

"Doctor, I'm Zack's mother." June said quickly.

"Miss Stapleton, your son has been diagnosed with a rare blood disorder, at the moment he is running a high fever which we need to stabilise, and then he will need a blood transfusion."

"What kind of disorder? How did he get it?" she asked in distress.

"We can't confirm anything at this point because we are still doing more tests." The doctor was noncommittal about a diagnosis which had June more anxious.

"So, no diagnosis?" June prodded hoping for more concrete information.

"However in these early stages, we need to do more tests to confirm a proper diagnosis in the meantime he needs a blood transfusion as his blood count has dropped significantly." The doctor was matter of fact but June was flustered.

What was really going on? No one in her family had any blood issues.

"I can do it, please take my blood for him." she begged wanting her son to get better quickly.

"I'm sorry but no close family member should give at this stage, since blood from a close relative may cause further immunological complications." Everyone stared at the doctor in surprise, feeling deflated that they could not help Zack.

"What does that mean?" June asked bewildered.

"Since we are unable to confirm exactly what is wrong with your son's blood, we want to explore all possibilities. So a precautionary measure at this stage is to avoid any genetic links which may cause an adverse reaction and that means no blood from any relatives." This news was not welcomed by the persons in attendance since they knew hospital reserves of blood were always low.

"Your son's blood type is A+ so we will scan our reserves to get him a match but if anyone here is not a family member that would also be helpful."

Dmitri stepped forward, "I am A+, I can donate."

Everyone looked at him in shock. June wanted to evaporate from the scene. Her family all looked at her in disbelief.

"You have not told him June?" her mother whispered angrily.

"I-I..." June stuttered. This was the moment she had been dreading ever since she found out about her pregnancy.

The doctor continued unfazed by the silence around him, "If this gentleman can give blood, his type is perfect, sir if you follow the nurse she will take you to the blood donation unit."

"Stop, you can't give blood, Dmitri," June came to him and held his hand stopping his exit.

"Let me help you June, I am okay to do this." Dmitri held her hand reassuringly. " I want to help."

"You can't." She said again.

"June please, I want to do this." Dmitri held her shoulders. " I no longer hate you June, let me help your son."

"You are Zack's father." June said in a rush. " You can't give him blood because he is your son."

Dmitri looked at her, his hands dropped from her shoulders to his sides as her words sank in. He just stood there and stared at her. The room was silent around them as they stared at each other. Dmitri's face was showing signs of revelation and acknowledgement as his brain appeared to be piecing together the news of being a father.

"I am O-, I can give blood." Franco came forward to break the tension filled air.

"I am O+." Gared ventured as well.

The nurse gestured to the two of them, "Please follow me gentlemen."

"Thank you." June said giving each of them a hug as they left.

"Well, umm, you can see your son for a short time before we prepare him for the transfusion." The doctor said nervously realising that things were quite tense at the moment.

"The parents should go in first." He added quietly glancing at Dmitri who was still frozen.

Dmitri had not moved since June's revelation. His body appeared to be in a sleep like state.

"You settle this now, young lady." Her mother whispered to her before walking away. Her parents were staring at her disapprovingly especially her mother. May and April gave her a comforting hug as she prepared to enter the ICU.

She tried to hold Dmitri's hand but he pulled away from her and walked past her to enter the room first. The nurse gestured for them to be suited up in protective wear. A nurse was checking Zack's temperature as they entered the sterilised room. The nurse smiled at them on her way out.

June rushed to her son's bedside and held his tiny hand. He looked so small and frail as he was hooked up to machines and wires. She looked back at Dmitri who was just staring at his son. She saw the muscles of his jaw tighten as he took in the whole scene; the room, the machines, the wires and the small delicate body breathing lightly on the small bed.

June let him have his moment; he walked close to the bed and held his son's hand, the huge one totally enveloping the other. Her son twitched, feeling the contact with his father. June wanted to die; she had denied her son his flesh and blood because of her own foolishness.

Chapter 21

It was early morning when she arrived at Dmitri's office building.

The elevator ride was long and treacherous as she contemplated her next step. She hoped that he would not throw her out in one of these humiliating scenes but she did not care. The man was insufferable. She was fuming. She knew that she had been wrong to withhold Zack's paternity from him but he had gone too far. She deserved whatever hatred he felt for her but right now she was desperate, forget pride, her son was more important. He had refused to pick up her calls and after hours of not being in contact with him she was on her last straw.

A middle aged woman who looked homely sat at a desk on the Executive floor.

June approached her and asked nicely, 'Is it possible to see Mr. Kanaredes?'

She asked politely with her hands shaking in fury;

'He has been in a meeting all morning, do you have an appointment, Ms....?' Mrs. Nikolos as her name plate stated asked,

June responded, "No, but I really need to discuss a matter with him urgently."

The secretary, smiled, "I'm sorry but Mr. Kanaredes is a busy person and you need to state your purpose and I will make an appointment and see if he can get in touch with you." Mrs. Nikolos looked at her expectantly.

"Where is Franco? His PA? It is urgent, get him out here now!" June was livid.

"If you continue to be disruptive I will have to call security." The secretary stated and went back to her typing dismissing June.

June did not care; her decorum level had flown out of the window nine hours ago when Dmitri had taken her son away. Her son was sick and he needed her to be strong now.

She turned around. 'Mrs. Nikolos, it is a matter of extreme importance that I see him can you call him out of his meeting?'

'Miss I already told you---'

'I need to see him, now!' she cut off the secretary.

Mrs. Nikolos picked up the phone and called security.

June ignored shouts to stop and rushed through the huge steel doors of Dmitri's offices.

She was beyond caring.

June kept her stance; she needed to see Dmitri before security got to their floor. She rushed to the first door and opened it, Mrs. Nikolos was shouting for her to stop but she ignored her. She pulled open the door but the room was empty. Franco Pavlis was written on the name plate on the desk. She was disappointed, but kept on she had little time.

She turned around and saw two uniformed security guards coming towards her. She dashed into the next room to her.

'What is going on here?' she turned around and saw Dmitri standing at the end of a conference table with several other people.

' I -- I-' she started as the door was again opened by the two guards followed by Mrs. Nikolos.

'We are sorry sir but,' explained Mrs. Nikolos, " she rushed in."

'June what is going on?' Dmitri asked her directly.

'I need to speak to you.' He looked at her for what seemed like an eternity, and then he nodded to the guards to leave.

'It's okay and gentlemen will you excuse me?' The seven men around the table stood up gathered their papers and exited with curiosity etched on their faces.

"Please hold my calls Franco," Franco looked at her apologetically, before he too made an exit.

When the door closed after the final person, June breathed deeply.

Dmitri was standing with his hands in his pockets. He was not wearing a jacket and his grey tie was slightly undone over his blue shirt which sleeves were rolled up to reveal his forearms.

"What is this about June, what are you doing here?" he asked seemingly angry by her interruption.

He was angry? She looked at him staring coldly at her. He had not spoken to her since that day she had revealed that Zack was his son. He had blatantly ignored her presence and avoided her like the plague and that was four days ago.

'Out with it!' he demanded as she stood there open mouthed staring at him.

'Where is Zack?' she asked softly clutching her bag tightly, her rage had been seething and she was barely holding it in. "I need to know where you have taken my son."

He looked at her and laughed, "He is being taken care of by a specialist team." Dmitri was very dismissive as he rounded the table and checked something on his tablet.

June could not believe how unashamedly rude Dmitri was being to her. Her family had cajoled her to go home for some rest and some downtime. She had reluctantly agreed as the test results had not come back and Zack was still in a medically induced coma. April had called her from the hospital about an hour later to inform her that Zack was being transferred via air ambulance. June had rushed to the hospital to find her son gone and no hospital staff were able to tell her where her son had been taken. She had been furiously trying to contact Dmitri all night to no avail.

He had changed his mobile number and he no longer lived where he had. She had been scouring the streets and the hospitals to find her son but with no luck. She had decided to come to his offices hoping he was there, to tell her where he had taken Zack. She had deliberately come to his office early to get answers and he was treating her like she did not need to know about her son. She knew he was angry about her omitting to inform his of Zack's paternity but this action was wrong he had gone too far.

'Dmitri this is not right! You can't just take my son away, not now, not when he is sick and needs me!" she shouted at him.

"I can do what I want June I am his father? Aren't I? I acted out in his best interest." He stared at her cruelly from his chair, 'You dare to come here, after what you did to me?"

She faced him bravely. 'Where is he?' she asked again this time her voice barely in control.

'You have every right to be mean to me Dmitri but not like this. You can't keep him from me; this is torture not being with my boy.' She was openly crying the tears were just streaming down her face.

Dmitri looked at her, his face hard and unreadable.

"Zack is being seen by the top blood specialist in the UK, he is under the best team to give a proper diagnosis until we know his true illness." Dmitri continued to look at his mobile, ignoring her presence.

"I have to continue my meeting this is my place of work. I will contact you if there is need." He looked at his watch and started to type into his phone. June could not believe the man. He was keeping Zack from her? How dare he make that decision on his own? She walked over to him and picked him his mobile and threw it across the room.

"If there is a need?!" she screamed at him.

"If there is a need!?" She picked up the tablet and also flung it at the window.

She placed her hands on either side of his chair and stared directly into his eyes.

"Tell me where my son is right now. This attitude of yours is exactly why I never told you about Zack before! This domineering and arrogant monster is what I do not want my son to grow up into!"

Her chest was heaving by the time she was finished. Dmitri pushed back his chair and she stumbled forward. She had to hold onto the table to prevent herself from falling onto her face. Dmitri stood up and approached her. He was like a tiger surveying his prey. He smiled at her, his teeth showing but his eyes were devoid of emotion. He stopped just in front of her and placed his hands in his pockets.

"I am a monster? After everything you still believe I am the monster? That I am wrong?" he tilted up her face and used his index finger to trace her upper lip.

"You destroy my property carelessly." he said pointing to the pieces of his phone and tablet scattered on the floor.

"So this monster is just good enough for what? Sex? With the almighty and chaste June Stapleton? You lied to me June for nine months you had several opportunities to tell me about Zack but you chose not to. After he was born you still kept quiet for a further eleven months." He was in her face suffocating her with his words of truth.

"You even had sex with me in New York but you did not tell me that I had a son, that I was a father, that my flesh and blood, my heir, my lifeline was in this world. And you dare to call me a monster!"

Dmitri walked away from her because he was so furious that he could not look at her any more. She was the mother of his son but he wanted to kill her right now.

'How dare you do this to me, June? How dare you? Deny me my son, keep him from me, he is mine and you took him away from me.' He continued, looking at her scornfully as he ranted. He was pacing but the look in his eyes were murderous. He approached her with his fists swinging; she cowered further into a corner. She had never seen anyone so angry. His whole body was tense and on fire. She stood there speechless as he raved in anger.

Dmitri pulled pictures from an envelope in his desk. He picked up the first one; it was of Zack at his baptism. He was dressed in a white short suit. He was four months old.

"Did I contribute to my son's name? No!" he put the picture down and picked up another one. It was of Zack standing in the park.

"Will I see my son walk?" he picked up another photo. "You better hope I do woman!" This one made June choke back her saliva. It was Zack at the airport waving her good bye as she had left for New York a week ago.

"Will he ever look at me or call me Daddy or smile at me?"

Dmitri came to stand near her again. "Answer me June?" he snarled at her.

"If anything happens to my son and he never recovers from this so be it June Stapleton I will crush you. I make your life a living hell for ever daring to deny me my son. You call me a monster then what are you? What kind of woman would do what you did and still dare to come in front of me with tears flowing down her face."

"I'm sorry, I'm so sorry." she sobbed, the words flowing out of her mouth as the tears flowed down her cheeks. She closed her eyes in pain as she realised the enormity of the situation? Was Dmitri going to keep Zack from her forever? Would she never hold her son again? Hear him call her 'Mama'?

'Look at me!' he demanded, 'Face me!' she slowly opened her eyes and looked at him. He was standing in front of her, the picture in his left hand and his right hand fisted against the wall beside her. She was trapped and afraid. Dmitri was like a loose cannon. She never thought that he would react like this and now she really regretted denying him the right to share their son.

"Please tell me where he is? I need him?" she pleaded making another attempt to softened Dmitri's cold heart, "I was wrong, I should have told you from the start but, please Dmitri don't do this to me? Zack is my son, I love him, and I'm his mother!"

"No, you are not a mother but a cruel and vindictive woman. A manipulative and deceitful person not a mother!" he had this real pensive look in his eyes which tore her heart in two, 'Now, almost two years later, you're telling me he is mine, and why? Because he is sick, sick enough to die!"

Dmitri backed away from her and ruffled his hair, as he paced around the room.

"Why? Why would you not tell me?" Dmitri's voice softened, he leaned against the desk. "Why would you keep this from me June after everything I have done for you? Am I that unworthy? Do you hate me that much?"

"Dmitri. I'm sorry, so sorry but I made the wrong decision!"

He looked at the picture again, touching Zack's face gently and lovingly, and then he spun round and gave her a lethal glare as he spat out the words,

'If he dies June I will blame you, it will be your entire fault, and his blood will be on your deceitful hands!'

He went to the desk and pressed a button on the phone.

"Franco bring in the documents." June was standing there still reeling from Dmitri's words. Her core was filled with so much emotional strain from Dmitri's words and the fact that Zack was being kept from her.

Franco entered with a large manilla envelope and gave it to Dmitri. Dmitri took the documents out of the envelope and scanned through them briefly before handing them to her.

"Read!" he commanded her.

She took the papers with shaking hands she dreaded what was in them. She looked at the title it stated Legal Guardianship of Jonathan Zack von Kanaredes.

She looked up at Dmitri in disbelief!

"No! You can't do this!" she screamed looking at the fine print which stated that the court had awarded Dmitri full legal guardianship of their son. She sank to her knees, the tears flowing; her pain turning into despair. He could not take her son away from her, not now. Zack was sick and she could not even hold him plus she had no idea where he was.

"Please Dmitri, no, please no!" she sobbed looking at the words on the documents in front of her.

"DNA tests conclusively prove that he is my son and due to my son's current state I am now his sole custodial guardian. If you want maternal rights I suggest you get yourself a solicitor." With that Dmitri left the room.

June remained there on the floor in shock. Her son was gone from her. She had no idea where he was and what he was feeling. He was sick and she could not be there for him. She was numb. She did not know how long she knelt there but after a while she stood up. Her body was numb and defeated. She walked out of the office building blindly unaware that people had been staring at her dishevelled appearance. She had hailed a taxi and headed home. She was operating on automatic pilot.

She entered Zack's room and held his favourite teddy. It was a stuffed build-a-bear of Makka Pakka from In the Night Garden. He had just loved the stuffed animal the first time he had seen him. June crumbled to the floor; she had not slept all night looking for her son. He had changed their son's name and taken control of him. He had taken her Zack away from her. She was being punished in the worst possible way. She did not deserve this! Yes she had lied to him but he had no right to do this!

June decided that she was going to fight for her son! She had to fight Dmitri but she would do it Zack was her child as well! She picked up her mobile and dialled a number she had not used in over three years.

Some Bryan Adams to ease the pain...Please forgive me!

Chapter 22

Sorry for the long wait before this update.... hope you like this chapter.

"June you brought this all on yourself!" her mother was still angry with her.

"This is not the time to finger point dear, we need to resolve this situation between the two of them!" her father stated diplomatically.

"I can't believe he would go so far!" May voiced. "Talk about venting his wrath!"

"Anger can make anyone do irrational things." April added.

They had all gathered at June's home for a family meeting on the way forward. April had made an appointment with one of the solicitors at her firm. They were awaiting his arrival.

"June have some chamomile tea." Her mother offered her. She shook her head, she had barely slept and she had no appetite.

"J please eat; you need to keep up your strength," April cajoled her. June shook her head again. Her mouth felt like cotton and her throat was constricted. The thought of food made her feel nauseous.

The doorbell rang and April volunteered to answer the door.

"This is Liam Watson." A tall handsome blond man came into view. He appeared to be in his early 40s. He was clean shaven and reminded her of the DA from one of those TV detective dramas.

"Please to meet you all." He shook their hands and he was guided to seat on the sofa.

"April has given me a summary of the situation and I have done some research." Liam was opening his attaché case and removing some files.

"Kanaredes is a huge corporation with a lot of influence in Europe to defeat him in the courts will be difficult." Liam stated something they all knew.

"I knew it!" her mother moaned. "I won't see my grandson again."

"However, there is chance we can appeal to a judge about your son's fragile state and that his chance of recovery would be increased by the interaction with his mother and family who he only knows. The inclusion of his father who is a stranger can cause him to relapse." Liam's words were not reassuring and June's heart just closed.

She burst into tears and May enveloped her into her arms.

Dmitri stood watching his son through the glass window in the adjoining room. The doctors had told him that Zack had a rare blood disorder and that he would need a bone marrow transplant. His son's little body was hooked up to many different coloured wires. He appeared stable at the moment but it was vital that he get a marrow donor before his blood poisoned him.

'Eat something Dmitri.' His mother's voice cajoled him. He turned to her voice. She had some food on a table.

'Mom, I'm not hungry.' He responded turning back to look at his son. He felt his mother's hands on his arm dragging him to sit at the table. He acquiesced.

'You need your strength, now have some warm tea.' His mother was adamant and he never defied his mother; so he sipped the tea slowly although his mouth had no taste for food.

' So what have the doctors told you about his condition?' his mother asked worriedly.

'They need to test as many family members as possible to see if they can get a bone marrow match.' He replied finishing his cup of tea.

"So when am I going to meet Zack's mother?"

Dmitri stood up. He had not told his mother about June fully. She had been ecstatic to know that she had another grandchild and had flown immediately from Sicily to be with him.

"Dmitri?" his mother came to him, "I know something is going on? You are my son and I know how stubborn you can be, so where is the mother? She must be worried for her son?" Dmitri turned away from his mother. He was still very angry with June for keeping Zack away from him.

"Well, she isn't here." He said not committing to say anything else.

"So did she just give you your son and run off when he was sick?" his mother was pushing and he did not want to go there.

"Not really." He said looking at his son through the glass again. He refused to think of June right now, if he did maybe he would be sympathetic but he was too furious to let himself think of her.

"Demetrious! I want the truth now!" his mother said firmly. He turned around slowly, his mother was a force to reckon with and he had no choice but to obey her.

"I took my son from her, she does not know where Zack is." He said quietly watching his mother's face change from disbelief then to anger.

"You took this precious boy away? Now tell me Dmitri was this woman evil? Did she want money? Was she abusing him?" his mother was prodding and he hated it. He ruffled his hair and started to pace.

"No." was all he said as he slumped against the chair. This was painful.

"I want to know it all." his mother's firm voice was a rod of discipline he had adhered to from a young child.

He told her everything and by the end of it all his mother stood up and looked at him firmly.

"As your mother I can only imagine the pain you must be feeling but to take her son away like you did is wrong. I know you are a ruthless business man but son how could you? We lost your father so young and it still hurts how could you even do that? You will undo this custody thing today."

"But-" His mother was speaking softly as she cut him off.

"You call this woman right now, I want to meet her. I want to meet the woman who has given me another grandchild." She was looking at him square in the eyes. "And the woman who has captured my son's heart."

June walked through the hospital doors briskly. The call she had received an hour ago from Franco was very strange but the fact that Dmitri was allowing her to see Zack was all she needed to get to the hospital very quickly. She had informed her family and although they had all demanded to come with her, she felt that she needed to do this alone first. Maybe

Dmitri had softened, she highly doubted it but this was a step. She would be with her son again. These past few days had been a living nightmare.

June entered the private wing of the hospital and saw Franco outside a private room. There were two burly looking guards dressed like secret service agents on either side of the door. June realised that she had seen a few of them in the reception area as well. Dmitri had always valued his privacy. She rushed to him.

"Is Zack in there?" she asked. He nodded.

"Is he okay? How is he?" she asked hurriedly so eager to see her son again.

"I will take you in now." Franco knocked on the door and June followed him as he entered the room. It was more of an apartment than a waiting room with sofas and a kitchen and what looked like a bedroom off to the side. Dmitri was standing facing the glass to another room in which there was a nurse and machines, she guessed Zack was in there. She could not see her son. There was an older lady sitting on the two seater sofa.

"Mr Kanaredes, Ms Stapleton has arrived." Franco said before exiting the room.

Dmitri did not turn around but the older lady stood up and came to her.

"Hello my dear, I'm Sofia, Dmitri's mother. You must be June." June extended her hand to the lady in front of her. She was about her height with dark hair and a firm grip. She was beautiful and had striking cheekbones. Her eyes could pierce you and June could see where Dmitri got his gorgeous looks from.

"I'm pleased to meet you." June said looking at Dmitri who still had his back to her. His hands were now in his pockets.

"Sit with me a while dear." June sat with her as the woman held her hands in her own. June was eager to see her son but she did not want to be impolite.

"I know you must be worried for your son and this situation is a bit awkward but my stubborn son over there was wrong in taking the child like he did." Dmitri cleared his throat but said nothing. June looked at her hands held by Dmitri's mother.

"Mrs. Kanaredes-"

"Please call me Sofia, let me finish young lady." This lady was firm. "Look at me, you were also wrong in not telling Dmitri about his son for whatever reason but two wrongs do not make this right." June was stunned. " This is no way for a son to meet his father." June knew that she was wrong, she was still agonising over it.

"I .." she was unsure what to say.

"You two need to be a united force for your son right now. He is sick and until he is better you two need to be strong for him together right now." Sofia von Kanaredes was indeed a resilient woman. She gave June a hug.

"Come on you must be eager to see Zack, we will talk more later." June got up and looked at Dmitri who was now staring at her. His face was blank but she could tell he was still angry with her by the way he held his shoulders. She approached him slowly.

"I'm really sorry for not telling you sooner. I really have no excuse." She said staring at the man in front of her with tears in her eyes. "Thank you for allowing me to see Zack again."

Dmitri said nothing as he stared at her for some time before saying.

"You can go in to see Zack now."

June got suited up and the nurse led her to Zack's bedside. She approached her son who was still in a coma. His small body was still hooked up to a few wires. She touched his face and kissed him through her mask. She then held his tiny hand.

"Oh my little precious one, I missed you. Mummy loves you so much."

Dmitri watched June with their son. There was no doubt that she loved their son. He watched them interact and felt badly about taking Zack away from her. She was tortured and maybe she was punished enough for her mistake.

"She is a mother Dmitri and their bond is strong." His mother commented watching the interaction with him. " You two need to forgive and move on for your son's sake."

A team of doctors were here to give them an update.

"Your son has a rare blood disorder. It appears he got a virus which affected his blood. Although the virus is now under control, the best thing to do is to strengthen the blood cells in his body against such attacks in the future." Dr Lassiter a haematologist was informing them.

"So what is the way forward to do this." Dmitri asked.

Mr Carmichael, the surgeon responded, "We need to have surgery and give him a blood marrow transplant. We hope that the inclusion of familial blood cells from a close family member who has at least 90% match will increase his resistance."

"We need to conduct a compatibility test on close family members to find a suitable donor." Dr Lassiter continued, "Then we will do the surgery, the recovery rate of this procedure is in the region of 60%, since your son is still young the rate is usually 75% for his age group."

"So the first step is for as many family members to do the compatibility test." Dr Lassiter stated.

"How long before you know the results of the tests?" June asked anxiously.

"It usually takes 3 to 5 days for the lab technicians to get the classifications but once it is done the surgery can be performed within a few hours."

"We want it done sooner." Dmitri demanded. The doctors looked at each other.

"Mr. Kanaredes, we want the procedure to be as accurate as possible, we can speed it up but it has to be done properly to ensure we get the best possible match for your son." Mr Carmichael ventured.

"When can we start doing the tests?" June asked eager to begin the process.

"We have already made arrangements for the lab to welcome the family, so the lab technicians will lead you to the lab for the tests to be done."

June waited nervously for the results. Dmitri had gone in first. The procedure was very simple but the wait was gruesome. May was in the test lab at the moment. Both paternal and maternal grandparents had done the test. Dmitri's sister Eva had flown in to do the test as well. She was a female version of Dmitri. She was a bit like April and the two appeared to connect quite well. Eva was married with two daughters. She was an accountant and owned her own firm which she ran with her husband.

The mothers had hit it off well. The two were currently rearranging their lives and June and Dmitri had no say in the matter. Dmitri had barely spoken to her and was speaking more to her family than to her. The team of doctors returned two days later with the compatibility tests results.

"So am I a match Dr. Lassiter?" June asked eagerly.

"I'm sorry Ms. Stapleton but your match is only 60%, we needed a higher match." June crumbled at the news. He father reached out and caught her before she fell. She started to sob.

"Of all the persons who tested Mr Kanaredes is the closest match of 91%, we are quite pleased because anything over 90 % is a positive sign. So we can proceed with the marrow donation as soon as possible."

Dmitri hugged his mother, "Great, I am ready to donate now."

"Dr Conrad, the anaesthesiologist will get his team ready to get your son prepared for the surgery." Dr Lassiter informed them.

"A syringe will be used to remove bone marrow from your hip bones Mr Kanaredes. Although this is not a surgical operation, you will be put under a general anaesthetic to stop you feeling any pain during the procedure." Dmitri was looking very emotional and June wanted to reach out to touch him but she knew he would probably push her away.

"You will usually need to stay in hospital for up to 48 hours to make sure you have recovered fully from the general anaesthetic." Dr Lassiter continued.

The wheels began. Dmitri did not acknowledge her but kissed his son before he left. Her mother came in and hugged her lovingly feeling her anguish.

'It's okay honey, he hurts just like you do, and it will be okay.'

June did not want to leave her son's side so she remained at his bedside until they wheeled him into surgery.

The Dr Lassiter told them that Dmitri's procedure had gone on well but the recovery part was not over yet. Dmitri was still unconscious and Zack was still in surgery with Mr Carmichael.

June went to Dmitri's room. He lay there so handsomely on the bed.

Eva was sitting with him.

"You can come in June, it's all right." June hesitantly entered.

"I'm sorry for interrupting." Eva invited her to sit next to her.

"I know things are a bit tense between you two but my brother has always been stubborn but family means a lot to him so he is just angry but it will wear off. Hang in there." Eva said.

"I hurt him badly Eva, I should not be forgiven, maybe all this is my punishment." June was tearfully this whole situation had tore her down mentally and emotionally.

"June do not blame yourself these things happen, you need to be positive."

"How do you feel about him?" Eva asked her directly. She had always denied what she felt for Dmitri but all the events of these pasts few days had made her reflect on her true feelings.

"I'm not sure, he makes me feel things I have never felt before, when I am with him it is like…. I'm complete, I loved our interactions and I loved to defy him." June said looking at Dmitri laying so serenely on the bed.

"Tell him." Eva encouraged her as she gave her a hug and then left the room.

She walked over to him, and brushed a lock of hair off his forehead. Like this he was so calm, she touched his cheek lovingly.

'I am so sorry Dmitri for all this, you are right I am to blame for selfishly keeping our son from you.' She paused ' I was so ecstatic when I found out I was pregnant, it was the same day that, I found out who you were, I was so angry, with you then. But I still wanted you so much. I lied to keep you away from me from capturing my heart.' she stopped her voice choking.

'How could I want someone who had treated me so badly. That day I lied to you about Zack's paternity I will never forget it. I wanted to take the words back then and there but I was too full of pride. When saw you again in the street I hated the look you gave me I wanted you to look at me with love pregnant with your child but I ruined it.'

She touched his nose, which was so much like Zack's.

'Zack is so much like you, he has your nose, your hair even your temper' she laughed softly.

'He enjoys food like you do, I think he is going to be wonderful cook.' she was smiling through her tears. She loved this man, she had never stopped. she traced his jawline loving the touch of his skin.

'He even has the birthmark on his bum like you, I am so sorry for keeping you from him I would like you to love him as I do and to play with him, I will never keep him from you again.'

She held his hand, "I promise you that if we survive this I will not keep you from him, ever. He deserves to have you in his life."

His hands twitched slightly; she froze, she didn't want him awake just yet. She was not sure if she could face him just yet. she was admitting her feelings for the first time and this was very new to her.

After a second he made no more movement she calmed,

'Zack should be finished now I will go and check on him, I never stopped loving you Dmitri, I don't think I ever will.' she kissed him lightly on his mouth.

Chapter 23

I figured I upload two chapters since I made you guys wait so long. One more chapter and it will end. Thanks for reading!

Zack was out of surgery, the doctor was hesitant to say anything, and he just said that they had to wait. She looked at her son through the glass door unable to comfort him. Her heart wrenched. She stood there for ages until her mother pulled her away to eat something.

"You need to eat June, how can you be strong for Zack if you too are weak." Her mother pleaded with her.

She took the sandwich and sat down,

"Here is some juice, J." May offered. June smiled at the persons gathered in the waiting room. Her family had been a rock of support and she knew that their strength was helping her to pull through this tough time.

"Thanks sis." She said trying to smile but it was small. She had no appetite and barely registered the sandwich she was offered. Her heart was torn. Her son was in recovery and so was his father.

Sofia and Eva walked into the room. They had probably come from visiting Dmitri who still had not woken up yet. Eva looked at her and smiled. Eva was the only one who had heard her confession to her brother.

"How is he?" she asked them.

"He will awaken soon, my son is resilient plus he is too much of a workaholic to be lying in bed for so long." They laughed knowing she spoke the truth. Although Dmitri had been in the hospital waiting with them, poor Franco had been busily taking orders and doing business from the adjoining room which Dmitri had set up like a mini office. He had a knack to set up office anywhere.

While the others mingled, she decided to check on Dmitri to see if he was awake. He was more than awake he was dressed and putting on his shoes when she walked into his room.

'What are you doing?' she asked surprised to see him dressed.

'I am not sick.' he stated matter of fact.

'You can't be released as yet Dmitri, the doctor said 48 hours it's only been a few hours, you need to rest more.' she insisted but he ignored her.

'Is Zack awake yet?' he asked pointedly.

'No he is in recovery, the doctor was non committal about anything.' she added

'I want to see him.' he was pulling a jumper over his head.

'Okay, are you sure you're all right?' she asked concerned that his colour was still a bit pale.

'Fine.' was all he said as he moved out of the room.

She followed him sedately, he was still angry with her. He walked into Zack's room and everyone stopped talking.

"Dmitri what are you doing here?" Sofia asked concerned.

"I am fine mother." He said holding her hand but he kept walking toward the glass to observe his son.

"You did not need to come so soon we would have told you if Zack was awake?" Eva added

"I needed to see for myself, I did not want to miss anything since I have already missed so much." He added firmly and June's heart twisted a bit at his dig.

"Dr Lassiter said by tomorrow Zack would be awake since they have reduced his sedative and hope to have some feedback on his progress tomorrow morning." June said.

Dmitri looked at her and excused himself to his adjoining office. The cold stare he gave her was still unnerving.

April gave her a hug and she tried to settle. The day wore on and June was restless. Everyone had gone home to rest. Sofia and Eva had gone to Dmitri's new home in Knightsbridge. Apparently he wanted a more family home and this one even had an indoor swimming pool, gym and sauna. The perks of being a billionaire. May had volunteered to stay with her in the hospital. Dmitri had been coming to see their son intermittently but she had not seen him for a few hours now.

She glanced at her phone it was half past midnight. May had fallen asleep about 45 minutes ago but June could not close her eyes as yet. She nervously waited for Zack to open his eyes and say "Mama!" she missed his smile and his laughter. She loved it when he was eating and made a mess everywhere; he wanted to be independent at his young age. She missed holding him in her arms and reading him a bedtime story. She needed her son to be alright, he had to be.

She sighed thinking that this has to work, the surgery had to be successful, if it didn't... she would not think of it, it had to; she loved Zack so much he was her life, her joy. A tear slipped out and rolled down her cheek. She was not going to give up and she was willing her son to fight, fight for life and for his right to live. She wrapped her hands around her body and closed her eyes as the tears fell freely.

Dmitri had been watching June cry. Her shoulders were shaking slightly. He was tired. He had finally let Franco go home to sleep. He was in the middle of selling one of his subsidiaries to the workers and the deal was proving to be trickier than he thought. The Chinese government were pushing for him to pay more tax. He refused to give in since that would only encourage them to do it again. They had finally agreed on satisfied terms and he was happy. He could relax a little bit and focus more on Zack.

The past weeks had been tough. Finding out that he had a son and then knowing that he might never see him smile or watch him grow was even more heart breaking. He had been furious with June but watching her in pain as well had softened his hurt. They were both suffering and he was happy that their families had banded together so well. He was surprised she was not sleeping, but then again neither was he. He wanted to reach out to her but he kept back until his body walked over to her maybe it was time to let her back in after all....they were in this together as parents.

Dmitri came to stand behind her; he squeezed her shoulders lovingly and she leaned back into him. He pulled her into an embrace, holding her body tightly against his. She held onto his hands as they formed a protective cocoon around her. They stood like that for ages each feeding off the other willing their son to fight.

Zack did not wake all night long but his condition did not worsen which was a positive sign that his body was accepting its new tissue. June woke up in Dmitri's arms; they were reclining on the sofa. Dmitri was stretched out on the sofa and she was lying on his body as his arms embraced her. Somehow, they had reached a truce although no words had been spoken. She snuggled her head more unto his chest until she realised that his breathing pattern changed.

She tried to pull out of his embrace to find him staring at her.

'Morning.' she said shyly looking at him with a smile.

'Morning.' he replied softly not releasing her from his arms.

She unconsciously reached forward to push back his hair from his face and pulled back her hand quickly after realising what she had done. She stilled and tried to sit up but he kept her locked in his arms.

'I heard you yesterday.' she opened her eyes widely as she stared at him, 'When I was recovering I heard everything you said.' Dmitri revealed and she remained still. He had heard her?

She bent her head, 'I was wrong to blame you,' Dmitri continued, 'I was hurting and I needed to make you hurt like I was.' she was speechless; Dmitri was apologising and forgiving her. 'What happened to Zack wasn't your fault; I don't want you continuing to blame yourself.'

She opened her mouth to speak and he kissed her, it was just a brief peck on her lips.

"I love you June, you somehow got into my heart and you are the mother of my son," June was in shock. Did Dmitri just say that he loved her?

Tears came tumbling down from her eyes, he wiped them away.

"You forgive me?" she uttered her mind still reeling from Dmitri's revelation.

"I love you and yes I forgive you, I hope you can forgive me for being revengeful."

June held his face in her hands, "Oh Dmitri I love you so much and-" he cut her off as he captured her lips with his. She opened up to him hungrily as she let all the pent up emotion spill forth. This felt so good. Dmitri was holding her and kissing her so passionately that she forgot everything else. She threaded her hands through his hair as he pulled her closer to him. The clearing of a throat beside them, sprang them apart like guilty teenagers.

May stood watching them with a cheeky smile on her face, "You two finally make up?" she asked, "If I had known I would have gone home and let you two have the bed."

June scrambled to stand up, her face flushed and red as she was embarrassed that her sister had found her in Dmitri's arms. Dmitri looked unruffled as he remained on the sofa and smiled at May conspiratorially.

"I better wash up." May said, walking towards the en suite "I'll be in there for around twenty minutes." May said giving them a wink before she closed the bathroom door.

June became self-conscious when May left. She rushed to the glass to look at Zack. His fragile body was breathing on its own. The monitor was beeping regularly which showed that his heart rate was stable. She hoped he would open his eyes soon. Dmitri enveloped her in his arms. She leaned into him as they watched their son together.

Dr Lassiter and Mr Carmichael came to see them later that morning.

'Your son is responding to the tissue transplant.' The specialist doctor said matter of fact. The family had gathered once again to hear the good news.

'Great, when will he be awake?' she asked unable to contain the joy bubbling inside her. Her son was going to live; he was going to be all right.

'We slowed down the sedation yesterday so he should awaken later today.' the doctor added carefully.

"When do we know if the transplant is truly working?" Dmitri asked pulling her into his embrace where she felt so secure.

'We will keep him under observation for the next few weeks but by the end of a five day period we will know for sure.' Dr Lassiter ventured. "But nothing is certain and we just have to take each day as it comes."

June was just so happy. Zack would be fine. He had to be. She gave Dmitri a hug and he returned it. Their families watched them curiously wondering what had happened overnight, the two had been barely speaking the day before and now they appeared joined at the hip. May gave April a wink and Eva smiled. They were happy for their siblings.

Around four o'clock that afternoon Zack opened his eyes; they were so blue and so alive.

'Oh my baby' she cried as he stretched out his hand to her. He was still connected to wires but she held hugged him gently.

'Mama' he said softly trying to smile.

'Yes mama is here,' she was laughing and crying at the same time. Her son would be okay.

Dmitri stiffened beside her, he had a look of uncertainty and relief on his face.

'Honey, there is someone I want you to meet,' she held Zack's hand and put it into Dmitri's own, 'This is your daddy Zack,' the two looked at each other an assessing look on their faces. So similar and so exact.

Dmitri was bemused and Zack looked the same way until he said, 'Dada.'

'Yes, I'm your Dada,' Dmitri bent and kissed his son's cheek. Zack put his arm around his neck, June started to cry. How could she have denied the two most precious people to her in this world, this moment, this love, this happiness?

'Dada.' Zack repeated and Dmitri started to laugh.

Chapter 24

I decided to just complete the story today...whew I feel good. It is great to have my first completed story on WattPad. Please leave your comments on what you thought of the storyline.

'Where are the glasses?' asked June's mother, she was busily searching through the kitchen cupboards.

'Mom, we have enough glasses, why don't you just sit down and relax.' June protested as she walked into the kitchen.

'You know I hate to be waited upon,' her mother protested.

'It's Zack's third birthday, Dmitri has pulled out all the stops, and the caterers will look after things.' Sofia came over to her as she touched her stomach lightly.

'You look like you need to put your feet up too.' Stated her mother lovingly.

'I will, later today,' she said thinking of lying in her husband's arms.

"So after the cake how will we serve this dessert?" the two mothers were busy discussing the arrangements that had already been made.

June moved out of the lavish kitchen and into the back yard of their home. She and Dmitri had married two years ago in a small ceremony and she and Zack had moved to Sicily with him. She loved the tranquil life but always made time to return to her family in London.

Her family had flown in a few days before and had been pampering Zack mercilessly.

She looked at the guests milling around the yard. Their home was huge but beautiful overlooking the beach. There were relatives from both sides of their families. Eva and her family were there.

"Shouldn't you be taking it easy?" Eva asked as June approached her.

"I will when this day is over." June responded laughingly. Her feet were already aching her. Eva's husband Marius and her two kids seven year old Gianni and five year old Leah were great playmates to Zack. They were currently running around the garden playing with cars.

"Hi Dad." She said approaching her dad chatting with her sister April.

"Hey beautiful, shouldn't you be resting?" her Dad asked concerned.

"June, come on and sit now!" April demanded of her.

"You can be bossy to your clients but remember I am still your older sister!" she said giving her sister a hug. "Help Mum out please she is going berserk in the kitchen!" April was now a certified barrister working for a prominent law firm, she was not dating and although her parents were making major hints in that direction April was more focused on winning cases than winning hearts.

'Mama!' Zack shouted. He had stopped treatment a year ago and six months ago he had been given the all clear, so far he had never had a relapse. The doctor said that he was fully healed and would lead a normal life. Now an active three year old he came running toward her in his navy blue short pants suit. He was looking more and more like his father every day. He barrelled into her legs full of energy and exuberance of any toddler.

'Dada says I can ride my car!' Zack totally treasured his father.

They had developed a firm bond between them. He literally had his father's blood flowing through his veins, the two were so similar in personality and demeanour, and she could imagine their bonding to last forever.

"Auntie May!" Zack shouted running to give her sister a hug.

"You made it!" she said embracing her sister who was staying in one of the guest cottages. " I thought I had to go down and drag you out of there!"

May had given birth two months ago to a little girl named Maya and June knew first hand that taking care of a newborn was not an easy task.

"I was ready ages ago but Mr Careful here had to check and double everything twice!" May was complaining as her husband walked to them with their daughter in his arms. "We are only coming to a party ten feet away from the cottage but he had to pack enough for a two week trip."

"Am I the only one who cares about preparedness?" Gared asked laughingly kissing his wife as they swapped their daughter.

"Never a dull moment with you two." June commented.

May and Gared were always squabbling but yet so in love; these two never agreed on anything except that they loved each other. No one had really been surprised when May and Gared had eloped a few months after she and Dmitri had tied the knot.

Gared picked up Zack who loved all the attention he was receiving.

"Are you having a fun at your party?" Gared asked in a soft voice twirling the boy around.

"Yeah, Uncle Gared!" Zack responded happily giving his uncle a big smile.

"Can I play now Mama?" Zack asked looking at his shiny new car as Gared put him down.

'Yes, you can, now be careful!' she warned but her son who had already ran off full of excitement.

He careered off into the direction of his bright red sports car that Dmitri had custom made for him. June smiled at her son who was now healthy and happy. She felt arms wrap around her waist and she leaned back into the supportive body of her husband. Dmitri kissed her neck as they rocked gently together.

'You have made his day!' she said lost in the comfort of her husband's arms.

"May and Gared welcome!" Dmitri stated acknowledging the couple next to them.

He had patched up with Gared, since they were both now family. In fact the two men got on quite well in spite of their history.

"Quite the party you have here Dmitri." Gared said looking around the garden filled with family enjoying the party.

"Indeed, a pity I can't have some wine!" May said longingly and Gared gave her a disapproving look.

"I better vet all your drinks or our daughter will be sleeping all day and night." Gared said worriedly.

"Would that be such a bad thing?" May responded, giving Gared a sultry wink.

"May!" Gared shouted shockingly. "Will you excuse us." He continued pulling his wife away.

June and Dmitri laughed at the couple who were complete opposites.

"Shouldn't you be sitting," Dmitri asked inquiringly rubbing her stomach gently.

"We have the whole night." June responded lovingly.

Their marriage was a happy one. They had been back to the cottage of their first meeting twice, in fact, they had now added a new memory there seven months ago. Dmitri was a totally, devoted husband and father. He ensured that his work didn't interfere with his time with his wife and son. She loved him completely. She did not have to work but Dmitri understood her need to do what she loved, so she did consultancy work now.

"This little one has decided to give me a reprieve for the afternoon." She said as their unborn daughter decided to move around in her womb.

"I guess she agrees," Dmitri said laughing and holding her tighter. "I love you and our family."

"I love you and our family." June repeated as they stood there enveloped in love and peace, looking at their healthy son, who was running around with shouts of glee and joy.

Their family was beautiful.

www.ingramcontent.com/pod-product-compliance
Lightning Source LLC
Chambersburg PA
CBHW072153407052G

44585CB00015B/1129